THE STOCK MARKET IS PREDICTABLE

THE STOCK MARKET IS PREDICTABLE

EXPLOIT PROVEN SEASONAL PATTERNS FOR HIGHER RETURNS

FRANCIS YEE

JJY PUBLISHING

FHY Systems, LLC

DBA: JJY Publishing

marketing@jjypublishing.com

Paperback First Edition

ISBN 978-0-9916502-0-0 Kindle Edition
ISBN 978-0-9916502-1-7 Paperback Edition
ISBN 978-0-9916502-2-4 ePub Edition

Cover Illustration Copyright © 2014 by Francis Yee
Cover design by Don Del, www.designs4ebooks.com
Editing by Ellen Falk, www.ebookeditingpro.com
Author photograph by Michele LoBosco, www.mlobosco.com

Typesetting services by BOOKOW.COM

To both my children, the driving force behind all that I do.

CONTENTS

Conventions and Notations

This book is for any investor, whether a newbie or an experienced investor. Many of the investing fundamentals and concepts are useful to you whether or not you choose to take that extra step and use the tactics explained in this book.

Many topics discussed in this book are so complex and involved that a separate book can be written about them. Such topics include tax laws and their ramifications on the individual investor. Others are Securities and Exchange Commission (SEC) policies that affect how investment firms operate. There are also many secondary and tertiary issues affecting the individual investor that are important to note.

These matters are brought up in the book to add context and clarity, but do not directly affect the central ideas. Another reason these secondary and tertiary issues are noted is that each one of us is in a different situation in our lives. While many of these side issues may not affect the vast majority of us, due diligence requires me to note them because some may be affected by them.

To keep you focused and provide depth and clarity on the central point while noting secondary ideas, the book contains side comments where applicable.

At certain points in the book, there will be headings in bold surrounded by brackets: **[Main Point]** When this is presented, I want to keep your focus on the points that are important to the thesis of the book.

A sample passage may be like this:

[Main Point] All tax-deferred registration account types have a penalty for early withdrawals. Depending on the investment instrument and the registration type, there may be restrictions on how the money is used. However, there are no tax or penalty consequences using the tactics and strategies in this section.

In this example, I felt compelled to note some of the tax consequences that have a monetary impact relating to the general topic.

Another is: **[PMMWMMI]** This is an acronym for "Putting My Money Where My Mouth Is."

My comments under this notation are to tell you what I have done, am doing, or plan to do within my personal portfolio.

A sample passage may be like this:

[PMMWMMI] I reallocate between Vanguard Fund X and Vanguard Fund A when the economy is slowing.

In the References section, I have cited the sources using MLA (Modern Language Association) standards. I have included a hyperlink to each source. Depending on which electronic device you are using or whether you are reading a printed copy of this book, connections to those web pages over the internet may not be possible. Instead of using a phrase such as "click here" or icons to embed the URLs, I have listed the actual URLs. Please keep in mind that web pages change constantly and the URLs may no longer be active. Use the MLA citations in your favorite search engine to find it.

PREFACE

To paraphrase, the stock market is not your father's stock market. Many things have changed regarding the stock market over the past thirty-five years since I've been trading and investing in stocks. These changes have a profound effect on our psyche as investors.

The proliferation of investment instruments provides such a dizzying selection that choosing the best ones is very difficult. Not only does this take time and require a full understanding of the investment instrument, but there are so many from which to choose.

Stocks

Now there are many more individual stocks from which the individual investor can choose. The Wilshire 5000, started in 1974, is the broadest stock market index and includes just about every publicly traded stock. Using the Wilshire 5000 index as a guide, there are now over 6,700 stocks tracked within this index. A diversified portfolio requires only fifteen to twenty stocks. To sift through all the stocks that are available is daunting for the individual investor like you and me.

Volatility

We hear about it just about every day. The stock market as measured by any index—Dow Jones, S&P 500, NASDAQ, Russell 2000, etc.—seems to move up and down in large ranges and by large percentages. It's been documented that volatility has increased since 1970. For the individual investor, this volatility increases our perception that stocks are risky investments—almost like gambling to some. This notion causes us to allocate too little into equities and more into cash-like instruments such as savings accounts and CDs. Unfortunately, these investment instruments earn very little and may not keep up with inflation. That is especially true over the past five to seven years.

Trading and Technology

The time from placing an order to completing a trade is fast and is measured in split seconds now. The old days when we placed buy and sell orders through market makers and the orders were recorded by pen and paper are almost gone. Almost all trades go through computerized databases and programs that connect to each other, even among the various stock exchanges. Long gone are the days when you called your broker to get a quote and had to make an instantaneous decision. If you waited to make a decision, you had to call again and hope he wasn't on the phone with someone else. Even when you placed a buy or sell order, you didn't know until much later whether the trade was executed. Today, click a few buttons and as long as your trade parameters (price, volume, and conditions) are reasonable, you'll get a confirming message or email within a minute, if not sooner.

International Stocks

Now, it is much easier to buy and sell them. Conventional wisdom is that we should have overseas stocks in our portfolio. If choosing individual international stocks is too complicated, we can still have overseas exposure through mutual funds or other forms of investment instruments. Some investment advisors are now suggesting that our portfolios should contain up to 40% in overseas exposure.

Mutual Funds

In addition to stocks, the proliferation of mutual funds from over 100 fund families is just as confusing and frustrating to the individual investor. He may hand over control of his investments to a paid third party. (Let's hope the person is a qualified investment or financial advisor.) I have many family members and friends who use an advisor. There's nothing wrong with using a qualified investment advisor if that is what you want, but it's a shame to do so just out of frustration.

Although mutual funds have been around since the mid-1920s, the proliferation of them didn't occur until the 1970s when there was a major shift from defined benefit pension plans to self-funded retirement accounts. Now there are over 10,000 mutual funds, with new variations offered constantly.

Recently introduced are Targeted Date funds. Retirement planning is the primary reason for these funds. These funds have a target year (retirement year) and will shift from a higher equity portion to a higher fixed-income (safer) portion as the target date gets closer. The philosophy is that as you approach retirement, there is less time to recover from major downturns in the market, so more money should be placed in less volatile instruments.

On the flip side of the coin, many of us may not have enough mutual fund choices in our company-sponsored 401(k) or retirement plans. And those that *are* offered may not be the best.

> [Main Point] Fidelity Investments is now offering similar date-targeted investments for 529 college plans.

Exchange-Traded Funds

One newer investment instrument gaining wide acceptance is Exchange-Traded Funds (ETFs). These are hybrids of mutual funds and individual stocks with certain characteristics of each. (ETFs are explained further in a later chapter.) The first ETF started trading in 1993. It was called the S&P 500 Depository Receipt (SPDR). In 2012, the number of ETFs had grown to 1,400. ETFs are gaining ground on mutual funds, but they still have a long way to go to catch up in the numbers offered and the amount of money invested in them.

There are many other investment instruments such as REITs, Options, Derivatives, and Commodities. After the meltdown in 2008, we all heard about how Wall Street bundled risky real estate loans into packages and sold them as investment instruments. These weren't even stocks. There was no ownership in actual companies. For this book, we limit ourselves to the three simplest and most popular investment instruments: individual stocks, mutual funds, and ETFs.

Individual Investing

How we invest has changed dramatically as well. The internet and the proliferation of computers to handle information and trade quickly have allowed the individual equity investor, like you and me, to gain more control over our investments. With almost every brokerage firm offering flat fees of around $9 per trade regardless of the amount or number of shares, there has never been a better time in the history of individual investing than right now.

In fact, unless you belong to a hedge fund or someone else manages your investments, you are the only one responsible for your investments. Even mutual fund companies and 401(k) administrators ultimately say *you* should invest based on *your* risk tolerance.

They offer a dizzying number of plans and explain the objective and risks, but it is *you* who must decide into which plans or funds to place your money. They do not suggest a particular fund. They can't because they are not offering investment advice.

The point is that you have much greater control of your investments than you may realize. But to effectively exercise that control you have over your own investments, understanding sound investment principles is vital. That understanding does not require a PhD. It does require making the effort to read, research, and understand some key principles and then using that knowledge to navigate through all the noise and headlines of the stock market to improve returns on your money.

CHAPTER ONE:
PATTERNS AND TENDENCIES

The stock market is made up of people—people who buy and sell stocks, and the collective whole we call the stock market. With the exception of programmed trades and the occasional typo on a trade, one single trade or trader will not move the market very much in a single day or over a long period.

The market can also be viewed as some organic entity comprising individuals and institutional traders who act independently of each other. The collective whole forms this organism that moves randomly.

It is a collective whole, *but it does not move randomly*.

The stock market is influenced by multiple factors. What it does on any day or in the short term is random and cannot be predicted. However, with the influence of tax laws, investment management practices, and predictable human behavior, the long-term investor can use certain investing tactics within a long-term investment strategy to improve investment returns that take advantage of proven patterns in the stock market.

Let's use lunch to illustrate the point:

It's been a busy day at work and you are looking forward to a break for lunch. You generally go to lunch around noon, but you may not for various reasons. You sometimes bring a lunch with you, but most often, you tend to buy lunch. You eventually choose to go out to a restaurant and not buy from the food truck outside. Although you have a wide range of foods to choose from, you decide to eat Italian today. Of the several Italian restaurants nearby, you choose Joe's Italian Eatery. By the time you get there, it is 12:25 pm.

Let's look at what just happened. You made a decision this morning, consciously or unconsciously, not to bring a lunch. Since you did not bring a lunch, you'll have to buy one today. Until the last moment, you did not decide where to go to eat. You eventually chose to eat lunch at a restaurant and not at the food truck conveniently parked outside. But it was probably predictable that more often than not, you will go to a restaurant. For whatever reason, you probably have a tendency, like most people, to eat at a sit-down restaurant than eat from a food truck. Continuing, you chose Italian. Was it predictable *today* that you would eat Italian even though you like a wide range of foods? Probably not; but over a period of time, your tendency to eat Italian food is predictable.

Now let's look at it from the restaurant owner's perspective:

The restaurant owner makes business decisions based on tendencies and the patterns they create. She does not know if *you* will come today and what you would order if you came. Based on patterns she's observed, however, she does know approximately how many people will come that day and what they will order. She knows this society (or any society) has a tendency to do certain things driven by laws, company policies, customs, and human behavior. These tendencies are predictable, and she will be correct a majority of the time. She needs to understand these tendencies and the patterns they create to run her restaurant profitably.

The time she opens the restaurant and how she staffs it is based on the tendencies of people's behavior during their lunch break. (We'll assume she does not serve breakfast.) Based on the tendencies she knows, she schedules the kitchen staff early to prepare the day's menu. But she does not schedule food servers to work until closer to the noon hour because she knows the tendencies of her customers do not to arrive until 11:00 am. There may be some customers who will come earlier because they are hungry, or they started their workday sooner than most. But the restaurant owner cannot make a business decision to staff more food servers and open the restaurant earlier just to service a few customers. She sets her opening hours based on patterns that maximize her profits.

She instructs her kitchen staff to prepare only a certain amount of food for lunch because she knows people tend to stop coming to her restaurant beginning at 2:00 pm. She probably reduces her food serving staff at this time and uses the same type of patterns to plan for dinner, as well.

The restaurant owner's situation is analogous to the stock market in many ways. She knows people (the whole stock market—all types of traders) will have to eat. She does not know if a particular individual (a particular stock) will come to her restaurant, and if the customer does come, she does not know what that customer will order (the stock price). What she does know is that most people will come between 11:00 am and 2:00 pm and she schedules her staff accordingly. Based on her experience, she will know the approximate number of people who will come on certain days of the week. Maybe she expects more business on Fridays because this society has a tendency to pay on Fridays and people have more money to spend on that day.

The restaurant owner never completely knows any of these variables, but she will make sound business decisions based on the predictability of people. She knows people will take time away from work to eat because of wage or employment laws governing lunch and time off for lunch. She can predict when most people will come to eat. She knows this because of societal customs. In most western cultures, it is customary for most people to start work between 7:00 and 9:00 am. People need to eat, and they tend to eat every three to five hours. Based on this, it is predictable that potential customers are hungry between 11:00 and 2:00 pm. Because of this tendency, she knows she must prepare for the lunch rush during that time period.

The same principles apply to the stock market. The pattern of having consistently higher-performing months along with the tendencies of investors are predictable a vast majority of the time. We will plan our investing tactics to take advantage of them.

CHAPTER TWO:
FUNDAMENTALS

Fundamentals

Fundamentals are the key to attaining wealth. There are two types, investing fundamentals and investment fundamentals.

Investing Fundamentals Are How We Invest

"Long-term investing" is a fundamentally sound approach. But what does "long-term" mean? Long-term means we invest under a philosophy of reasonably sustained gains to increase wealth over time. For tax purposes, long -term means holding investments for more than one year.

As long-term investors, we buy and hold investment instruments for a period of time that gets the highest return. There are two main ways to do this.

Choose investments that have strong fundamentals and continue to hold them until the fundamentals no longer exist. Buying and selling frequently will incur trading costs with each trade. Also, you cannot predict short-term movement of stocks consistently. You can, however, predict long-term movement because fundamentals drive long-term movement.

Pay fewer taxes and use that saving to earn additional money. Taxes decrease wealth. If an investment is for held for less than one year (bought and then sold within 365 days), then any gains will be taxed at the ordinary-income rate. The ordinary-income rate is the same rate as income from our jobs or work. If you are in the top tax bracket, that tax is 39.6%. However, if the investment is held one year or longer, any gains will be taxed at the lower long-term capital gains rate of only 20% for those in the highest tax bracket. See table 2-1.

These two go hand in hand when it comes to sound investing practices.

Table 2-1. 2013 Tax Rates

	Single File Status			Married File Status			Tax Rate	QD* & LT* Gain
Range:	$0	-	$8,925	$0	-	$17,850	10%	0%
	$8,926	-	$36,250	$17,851	-	$72,500	15%	0%
	$36,251	-	$87,850	$72,501	-	$146,500	25%	15%
	$87,851	-	$183,250	$146,501	-	$223,050	28%	15%
	$183,251	-	$398,350	$223,051	-	$398,350	33%	15%
	$398,351	-	$400,000	$398,351	-	$450,000	35%	15%
	$400,001	+	above	$450,001	+	above	39.6%	20%

QD*=Qualifying Dividend; LT*=Long Term

Tax Rate=Ordinary-Income Rate
Graphic Source: Adapted from Anspach, Dana.
"2013 Tax Rates—What to Know for Retirement." About.com.

The difference at the top tax bracket is 19.6%. Holding an investment for over a year saves 19.6% points off the tax on the gain. An investment bought and sold within a year must make a killing to offset this difference. Paying taxes at a higher rate cuts dramatically into returns already earned. Your tax bracket may be lower than 39.6%, but as you can see from the table, the savings are comparable at the lower rates too. But that's not the point. The point is that the difference between the tax rate for ordinary income and capital gains is so great that any investment has to return a much higher rate just to offset the difference in taxes. Having massive gains enough to offset the differential tax rate in such a short time would be fantastic. But you can't count on it happening often. For us long-term investors, we choose investment instruments that come out ahead over the sustained long run.

Your tax implications may differ. But the example clearly demonstrates how long-term investing, even just one year, makes a big difference in how much money you will keep, which translates to how much wealth you will have in the future.

[Main Point] Just lowering the tax impact from ordinary income to long-term capital gains is an important strategy that will significantly improve your long-term profits.

Investment Fundamentals Are What, How, and Why We Choose an Investment

There are many types of investment instruments. Some can be complex and risky. Long-term investors do not choose risky investments. The individual investor like you and me can be fully diversified in equities with just stocks, mutual funds, and ETFs. So we will focus this book primarily on these three.

[Main Point] Being fully diversified means having a mix of investment instruments where some go up and some may go down or stay level at any given cycle of the economy or under the same market conditions. The concept is to have a mix of low-correlation investments within a portfolio to balance high-performing ones against low-performing ones. It seems counterintuitive not to place all investments in high-performing investments. The problem is, we don't know when the high flyers will crash and burn. And we don't know when the poor-performing ones will rocket up. As investors, we minimize the risk by aiming to get steady, reasonable returns. The concept of correlation will be one of the cornerstones in our tactics discussed in Chapter Six.

Stocks

Stock-Choosing Strategies

There are many strategies for choosing stocks based on every conceivable matrix or idea. I've come to the conclusion that no single one is highly accurate because, if there were a proven method, there wouldn't be so many still around.

The following is just a short list of the most frequently used strategies or ideas. I have not gone in depth into their explanations because they are not important for us. You don't need to fully understand them. I listed them to give you an idea what other traders and short-term investors consider when trading stocks.

There are investment strategies that look at what other traders are doing and do the opposite. Traders who use this strategy are called Contrarians.

The opposite of these traders are the Momentum players. They look at the direction a stock has been traveling and go along for the ride. They sell when they think the stock has reached its peak and they wait to buy until they think the stock has reached its bottom.

Value investing is looking for stocks that seemed "undervalued" or have a stock price that is lower than what an investor thinks the price should be.

Growth investing pays attention to the growth potential of a stock. Less weight is placed on the current valuation of the stock's price at current levels.

Technical analysis uses points plotted on a graph to determine the future movement of the stock price over a set period. The following are some examples:

Trend Line Analysis

The graph in Figure 2-1 plots closing stock prices and connects them to show the high and low closing prices. Then two parallel lines are drawn near the top closing prices and near the bottom closing prices over a given time period. These two lines represent the buy or sell points.

Figure 2-1. Support & Resistance Trend Lines

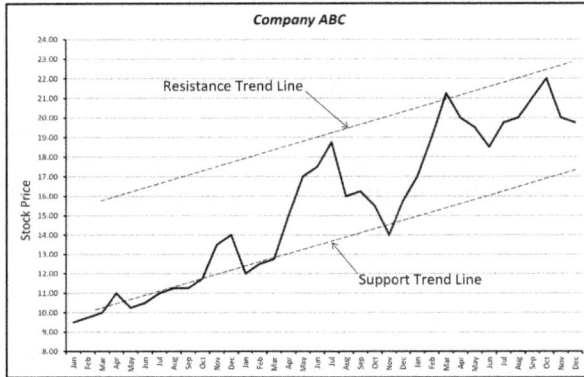

Source: Adapted from Wikimedia.org.

Regression Analysis

Regression analysis also plots the closing price of the stock on a graph but draws a line through the mean (or average) price of the stock to show the projected trend as to how high the stock price may continue to rise.

Chart Patterns

Still other strategies look at chart patterns and the shapes they create when the stock price is plotted on a graph. There are many theories as to the meaning of each pattern. Some patterns are for long periods, while others try to glean some significance within a trading day. The following few will give you an idea what those charts may look like.

Many of the strategies shown above base their investment decisions on what the stock price is doing at any given time. Often, this is done with little or no

Figure 2-2. Regression Analysis

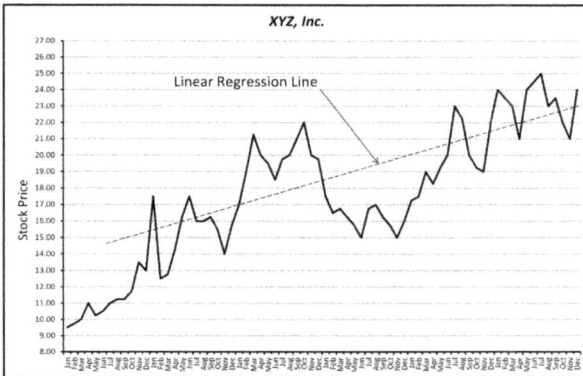

Source: Adapted from Stockcharts.com.

Figure 2-3. Head and Shoulders

Source: Adapted from Stockcharts.com.

regard to investment fundamentals of that particular company. The only time when the price matters to you, as a long-term investor, is when you've already made your decision to buy or sell the stock *after* careful consideration of the fundamentals. Only then should you determine when in the near future is the right price point to enter or exit.

Some of these investment strategies have a place as *part* of an overall decision

Figure 2-4. Cup and Handle

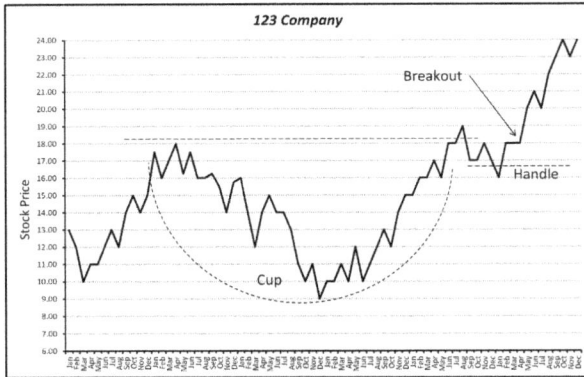

Source: Adapted from Stockcharts.com.

Figure 2-5. Candle Stick

Source: Missingstep.com.

whether to buy or sell a stock at a particular price. Many do not.

The Right Way to Choose Stocks

Choosing a stock isn't that hard for the individual investor. With the internet and all the information that's available through many websites, access to research and sound investment advice is only a few clicks away.

When you buy a stock, you are buying a part of that business. Start by picking a company or product with which you are familiar. Do you use that product? Do you like it? If so, then invest some time before you make a purchase. Choosing a quality stock requires research, attention to details, and patience. Choosing a stock is an exercise in thinking. It is not an exercise reacting to emotions.

Let's look at some of the major considerations when choosing a stock.

The Company

Often the company and its name recognition are reason enough to consider the stock. If it is a large corporation that the general public is familiar with, it probably has been in business for a long time and has developed a good reputation for its product or services. The exception is if the company or company name has been sold to a new group of investors or management team. Often the product or service is very different from what the original brand name was and the new management team or owners are new and most likely will not have a proven track record. Some recent examples are Hostess Foods and SAAB.

However, what the company is doing today is more important. Is it continuing in the same course that has made it profitable and viable all these years? Is the company selling the same products and services that have created a brand name over the long term? And do you believe this company produces a great product and will support that product? If you answered yes to these questions, then this is a good starting point that this company's stock may be worth investing in.

The company's financial situation is very important. You don't have to read all the financial statements, annual reports, and SEC filings that the company produced. The information contained in these documents is very important. But instead of reading them yourself, unless you have the time and you can understand what's contained within, seek out information and opinions from trusted investment websites and authors to hear what they are saying. Research the news. One obvious point to look for is whether this company is making money. Look to see if they had been making money consistently over the past five to ten years. See if there is a sustained growth or consistent earnings throughout this period.

Look for any information that talks about debt for this company. Did they have to raise more money through issuing new stock? Are they engaging in a joint venture? Or have they simply been incurring additional debt? The next question to ask is: how is this additional money to be used? Is it for research and development, capital improvements, or any other outlays that will help the company grow in the future? If yes, that may be a good sign because these monies are investments by the company for future profits. It also shows the company is looking toward the long term. If the money borrowed is for maintaining operations, that is not a good sign. Sometimes solvent companies have to borrow money if there is a delay in production, unexpected costs for manufacturing and services, or there was just a temporary delay in receiving money from customers. These short-term cash needs occur occasionally in businesses. If this happens often or there is no specific reason the company has to borrow money to maintain operations, this is not a good sign to invest in this company's stock.

See if there's been talk in recent articles about the solvency of the company.

If you see any information regarding any impropriety of the company's books or financial statements, do not purchase the stock. If you already own the stock, be prepared to sell it. Any hints of problems with accounting practices will surely set off investigations by the SEC and multiple stockholder lawsuits.

Often, it takes years to resolve these matters. If it turns out there were inappropriate accounting practices or misstatements in the financial reports, the stock market and investors will punish the stock. These are unjustifiable risks in owning the stock.

Management

Management is one of the most important factors in a company's success. You've probably heard of the phrase, "they ran the company into the ground." You can have a great company and a great product. But without sound management to maintain the profitable course as well as having plans for the future, what once was a profitable company will soon stagnate and will lose out to its competition.

When choosing a stock, see if current management has been effective in continuing its profitability and has a vision for growth. Look for any difficulties the company may encounter in the near and distant future. Such problematic issues may be newer technologies and manufacturing processes that will compete with or potentially make current methods obsolete. Some examples are Beta vs. VHS, land-line phones vs. mobile phones, PCs vs. Smartphones and tablets, traditional manufacturing vs. 3D printing, and hardbound books vs. eBooks.

If there are difficulties, what is management doing about them? Are they diversifying their product lines and increasing revenue through other means by creating a wider moat (more on this later)? Are they adapting the newer technology?

If there is a patent or some exclusive right to manufacture or market a product, see how the company plans to use that exclusive right and how strongly any infringements by other companies will be defended. Some examples are Samsung vs. Apple, major drug companies vs. generics, Bratz dolls vs. Barbie.

Look at the top management team. (Often, the spotlight is on the CEO. After all, he or she is the top person and he or she chose the people who will implement his or her strategies and philosophy.) Succession is very important. See if the company has a program or has acknowledged that a succession plan is in place. There is constant talk about Warren Buffet's successor. There was much talk about Steve Jobs' successor. Ask yourself if Jobs' successor has been successful. The jury is still out regarding Tim Cook. Apple is a clear example that a good successor is important to the long-term viability of the company. This should be considered in your decision whether to buy the stock.

Without a secession plan or qualified people currently in place, the company will have to look outside. The track record is spotty when a new senior executive has to be brought in. Often, the reason the company goes outside is that it is not performing well. Whether it needs "new blood" for a new direction or a "white knight" to salvage the direction of the company or a "fixer" to start from scratch, all bodes to the fact that current policies are not working. Generally, a company does not seek out senior management if it is performing well. Why did Yahoo! seek out Marissa Mayer? It was not doing well, and previous shakeup attempts from internal management were not effective in turning the company around.

Bringing in new management is no guarantee a company will improve its situation. As of this writing, the consensus on Wall Street is that Ms. Mayer has yet to improve Yahoo! in any appreciable way. In fact, on January 16, 2014, it was announced that Henrique de Castro, the chief operating officer Ms. Mayer convinced to leave Google Inc. in 2012 to join Yahoo!, is departing after only about a year on the job.

PetSmart announced in January 2014 that the CEO was retiring. There were other issues that affected the steep drop in the stock price, but the change in leadership was a major reason. The fact that there was a change is of no consequence for the long-term investor. Whether the change was anticipated, however, is something to consider. But most important is how the new leader and the new management team will affect the company going forward.

Many articles by respected magazines and writers are available on the internet. Visit news portals such as Google News and Yahoo!. They each have sections devoted just to finance where you can enter a stock's ticker symbol (or the company name). What will be shown, in addition to the current stock price, are news articles related to that particular stock. Many are just musings of bloggers. Just filter the noise and read the facts of the articles and then make a judgment whether any opinions are usable for your decision. Read through these articles and come to a general understanding of what the consensus is for the new management team.

Especially look for whether recent management decisions are questioned by the articles and why. See if the reasons are legitimate business decisions that have long-term or dire consequences. Try to understand the authors' reasons for specific points of concern. Are they legitimate or do they have an ulterior motive? Be careful, there are many writers out there who have a vested interest in what they say in public. They may be trying to influence the stock.

(After the meltdown in 2008, the Federal Communications Commission instituted new rules. Anyone expressing professional opinions on a stock(s) must disclose whether they own the stock(s); if they have a position in the stock (a buy or sell order); or whether they plan on taking any action on the stock(s) within the next 72 hours. During this time, it was documented that many independent bloggers and experts were paid. These people were paid advertisers pretending to be unbiased experts.)

Pay less attention to disenchantment with management decisions that affect the short-term price of the stock. You are a long-term investor; decisions that affect the ongoing profitability and growth of the company are more important. In my upcoming book, *Stock Market Noise*, we'll explore what is important and learn how to filter out unimportant noise that may actually hurt you.

Product or Service Strategy and Competition

One gauge of a company's strength is how its product or service is positioned in the market and how well it can fend off its competition. This is called a moat.

A moat generally has two components. The first is revenue stream. Does the company have multiple products or services other than just one main source of revenue? A company having more than one product revenue is considered to have a wide moat. Second, a company that is the leader or has a dominate position in the industry has a better chance of fending off competitors. This also adds to widen the moat.

Questions to ask are:

Has this company been the leader or has it had a dominant position in the industry for several years straight? An established large company usually is in a strong financial position to fend off competition. It has the corporate structure to make things happen from within and has the monetary resources to implement any production or marketing strategy. It may be strong enough to buy the lesser competition. Examples are Microsoft, Google, Merck, and Facebook.

Is the company a leader because of an established technology and manufacturing process? Usually leaders in established technologies and manufacturing processes enjoy a competitive advantage because the product is too costly for the competition to make, or the capital outlay is too great to enter the market.

Gillette is a good example. Anyone can make razor blades. But very few can make great razor blades cost-effectively. Gillette has the production methods and technology to hone sharp blades and sell them at completive prices.

Is there a new technology in the near horizon available to competitors that will make the current one obsolete? If there is, learn how the company will position itself for it. If the company does not seem to be adapting, be weary. Look at BlackBerry. They were the standard; the company dominated the market. Touch-screen technology made BlackBerry's technology obsolete. Yet the company had time to adjust and adapt to new technology, but it did not until it was too late.

Is this company introducing new technology? If the technology is new, then the company has an advantage over the competition. But the advantage will only last for a short time. A hot new technology is usually obsolete in a very short time. Some examples are DVD vs. CD, Wi-Fi vs. cordless; Facebook vs. MySpace, and tablet vs. laptop.

Is there a patent or some exclusive right to manufacture or market a product? A company that has exclusivity over a product or process is in a strong position over the industry. Imagine being able to make a product that no one else can. Remember one caveat noted above? There are two things that make a wide moat. Product domination is not enough; multiple revenue streams are also critical. The competition may not be able to make the same product, but if the company fails to stay financially viable, it may end up selling that exclusive right.

Large pharmaceutical are a great example of this. There generally is a 20-year period before generic drugs can be manufactured. But the company has to keep producing newer drugs continually to stay viable as a company.

Does it have other sources of revenue? Does it have other products that generate revenue? Are these other products similar or vastly different? See if the other source of revenue is horizontal or vertical. Horizontal is better. It means the other revenue streams are from different products that are not dependent on other products the company produces. They may be similar, but not dependent. Vertical is not as good. Vertical means that one product builds on another product for sales. Vertical streams are vulnerable because if there is a problem with a particular product along the chain, subsequent products will be affected as well.

> **[Main Point]** The product(s) or service(s) by itself is less important than how the company is positioned with consumers and competitors.

P/E Ratio

The P/E ratio (price-to-earnings ratio) has less to do with long-term profitability than the valuation of the stock price. This ratio tells you whether the current stock price is in line with its earnings projection for the near future. A P/E ratio of 12 to 18 is considered the optimal range for most stocks. This is not that important to you as a long-term investor. It only gives you an idea whether to buy or sell the stock at its current price. If you are close to deciding on buying a stock based on the fundamentals, then consider the P/E ratio to determine if the current stock price is a good entry point. However, if you believe you want to hold the stock for several years and expect it go up considerably higher than the current stock price, then disregard the P/E ratio and just purchase the stock.

Earnings and Guidance

A public company often has quarterly investor meetings open to the public. You can either attend those meetings via the web or just wait for the news to present the details. Pay close attention to the "guidance." This refers to whether the company expects its projections for sales or earnings to continue as anticipated or management has changed their guidance: good or bad. The stock market will usually react to any changes in the company's guidance. As a long-term investor, you should not react with the market. However, listen to what they say about their long-range strategy or what they say about their products or services. Listen for any mention of new technologies and competition. Listen for comments about the company's revenue stream.

Mutual Funds

Mutual funds are the cornerstone investment instrument for the vast majority of individual investors like you and me. Most investment instruments offered by company-sponsored 401(k) plans are mutual funds. When you buy mutual funds, you are essentially letting the fund manager do all the tasks noted above for you, and more.

But you'll have to choose the right funds to fit your investment strategy. Funds are mainly chosen based on their characteristics or objectives, which will be disclosed in the prospectus of that fund. The fund manager will pick stocks or other investment instruments based on the prospectus. The prospectus may specify what kinds of stocks can be bought and in what proportions. The mix of investment instruments may include bonds, money market accounts, or even just plain old cash. Some funds limit the percentage of cash held and may force fund managers to use that cash to buy stocks even when they do not want to.

The fund may purchase only U.S. stocks or only foreign stocks or any combination. Many international funds focus on just one region or the potential growth of the economies.

There are index funds that buy all the stocks in that particular index. [1] These funds try to mimic the diversity of that index and the objective is to just go up or down with the index. Other funds buy stocks that have growth characteristics or focus mainly on underpriced stock (value stocks). Funds may hold stocks in multiple sectors. Sector Funds accumulate stocks based on an industry or section of the economy.

Still other funds may buy stocks based on the size of the companies' total value such as large-cap, mid-cap or small-cap funds.

These are only a small list of the most common fund characteristics and objectives. Pick the ones that are most comfortable for you.

Costs

After choosing the investment objectives you want for your mutual funds, the most important consideration is costs. And there are lots of them. And you

[1] All non-index funds use some index to measure their own earnings against other funds to determine how well the fund is performing.

pay for them year after year after year.

Actively managed mutual funds have high expense ratios because trading expenses are incurred when the fund manager buys and sells stocks. Actively managed funds mean active trading and selling of the underlying stocks held by the mutual fund. The more buying and selling, the more brokerage cost the fund incurs. Also, research costs are higher because more stocks are analyzed.

Passively managed funds include index or fixed-income funds. There is little trading because index funds do not try to beat the index against which they are measured. As such, brokerage fees are much lower. Less research is needed since the fund only purchases the stocks in that index and in the same proportions. And compensation for the fund manager is lower since there are no major investment decisions to be made. Although fixed-income fund expenses may vary, they are lower than equity funds.

Costs to you as a mutual fund investor can be divided into two main groups.

Loads

This first group of costs is nothing but the privilege to participate in the fund, to join the "party" if you will. These costs are usually referred to as the "load."[2] Most "load" costs are usually paid when you first join the fund (front-load). These costs are deducted up front even before the remaining balance is invested for you. These "loads" are also called "sales charges," "commissions," "fees for salesperson." I call it "robbery loot."

There are also "back-end" loads. They are imposed when you sell. These loads are a little more involved in their calculations, but basically; they are costs to "leave the party"; I describe them as "bail" to leave jail.

There is no good reason to purchase load (front or back-end) mutual funds. The prevailing justification is that these funds are better managed and the returns

---

[2]The loads may vary depending on the class of the mutual fund shares. For us, the individual investor, Class A shares are what we generally purchase—without knowing it.

are much greater than other funds, thus justifying the load to participate in the fund. Baloney. There is no evidence for this claim. In fact, all evidence points to the contrary. No-load mutual funds perform just as well or better than load funds when the cost of the load is factored.

No-load mutual funds are the only funds you should own. There is a wide variety of them with enough different characteristics to meet any investment objective without having to choose a load fund.

> [Main Point] The perfect investment instrument for our upcoming tactics is no-load mutual funds. You'll see why when we get to that chapter.

Expense Ratio

The second group of costs to you is ongoing expenses incurred each year for the life of the fund or until you leave it. Expenses in this group are called the "expense ratio." The expense ratio, as the name implies, is a percentage of costs of the entire fund. If the expense ratio is 2%, then that percentage will be taken out of the total value of the entire fund. It is evenly distributed to all fund holders based on their portion. In other words, the cost to you will also be 2% of the value of your investment. You will never see that expense amount shown separately and distinctly on any statement. This expense is taken out by adjusting down the Net Asset Value (NAV) of the fund. The NAV is the value of one share of the mutual fund similar to the price of one share of stock. Most funds distribute dividends and gains by adjusting up the NAV at the same time or increasing the number of shares to distribute gains (both long -term and short-term) the fund accumulated. The total value of your fund doesn't show much of a change when this happens. You won't see the expenses distributed unless you are astute. Look for a big drop in the NAV in one day, primarily in the month of December.

The expenses in this second group can be broken out into three distinct types: (1) direct expenses, (2) general and administrative costs, and (3) 12b-1 fees (or marketing fees).

Direct Expenses

These expenses are directly related to the management and primary operation of the fund. The biggest chunk is fund manager compensation. Fund managers are paid on a percentage of the total value of the fund. The percentage is small, but multiply that to the total value of the fund and it's easily seven figures. I'm not pontificating on the compensation of fund managers in this book. I'm just laying out the facts. Other expenses include brokers' fees and other transactional fees directly related to buying and selling stocks (or bonds and any investment instrument held by the fund). Also included are expenses to research and analyze companies and stocks.

General and Administrative Costs

The expenses in this category are for items that are not directly related to selecting, buying, selling, and managing the fund. Such expense may include printing, copying, postage, delivery, utilities, office rent, office supplies, and equipment, etc.

12b-1 Fees

These fees burn a hole in my gut as well as my portfolio. These fees are outdated, unjustified, and superfluous. Mutual funds charge these fees for no good reason other than because they can and they get away with it.

These fees were approved by the SEC in 1980 under the premise that a mutual fund will become more efficient in its expenses if more people and more money are participating in the fund. To attain that end, mutual funds are allowed to deduct a certain percentage from the total value of the fund each and every year. The maximum allowed is 1%. Even "no-load" mutual funds can deduct up to 0.25% each and every year and still call themselves "no-load" funds. Now, with over 10,000 mutual funds and over $10 trillion in assets, this premise is outdated and the fees need to be changed or eliminated. In 2010, Mary Schapiro, chairman of the SEC, questioned these fees by saying, "We need to critically rethink how 12b-1 fees are used and whether they remain appropriate. . . ." Nothing has happened. Mutual funds still impose these fees.

What are these darn expenses, after all? No one knows for sure what expenses are in these 12b-1 fees. Funds have some latitude on how these fees are used.

The primary reasons are for marketing and sales commissions to get more people participating in the fund as noted above. There is no proof these fees are effective at doing so. Marketing expenses include advertising in various mediums such as printed brochures, newspaper ads, and television commercials. When you see a mutual fund commercial the next time, you'll now know that you paid for it with no evidence that it worked making your fund more cost-effective. Marketing expenses may include country club memberships, golf fees, and dining expenses to promote the fund. There are no definitive restrictions to how the fees can be used.

Also included are sales commissions to brokers (not the same as "load" fees). When you buy from a fund salesperson, planner, or financial advisor, that person gets a cut of the 12b-1 fees every year after the fund was sold to you. Even if you did the research and decided on a mutual fund with no help or guidance from anyone, the investment superstore that sold you that fund will still receive commissions through 12b-1 expenses.

The only way to avoid this fee is to read the prospectus very carefully. If a fund imposes this fee, it must state so in the prospectus. Eliminating this fee is worth the effort of reading the prospectus. Or better yet, ask the broker or financial planner if the fund has one. (Vanguard and T. Rowe Price have eliminated 12b-1 funds from most if not all of their mutual funds.)

[PMMWMMI] Many years ago when I was still learning about investing, I realized I was not good at picking individual stocks. I realized this in the year 2000, when I took a bath because all my investments were in high-flying tech and telecommunication stocks. Does the name Lucent cause anyone pain?

I decided to punt and invested in mutual funds exclusively. I thought, heck, I can choose the mutual funds myself. I thought just choosing the mutual funds was all I had to be concerned with since the fund manager will choose the stocks.

In hindsight, I also should have realized I was not good at picking mutual funds. I chose mutual funds in the same manner that I chose stocks. I chased after the hot funds that I read about in glowing testimonials and picked the highest-performing funds thinking they will continue at their pace. I did not pay attention to other aspects of mutual funds, especially the costs that were passed along to me.

Over time, I started learning more about mutual funds and their costs. I knew about the loads, but I thought, heck, since these funds were performing so well, the 6.5% load was worth it given the high returns these funds were getting me. So I continued my naive ways.

A few years later, when I left a job, I rolled over my 401(k) into a traditional IRA at another investment firm. I had to buy a new mutual fund because the new employer didn't offer the same fund as my last employer. I remember this very well, because the total dollar amount was very close to a nice round $10,000. By this time, I was very aware of the 6.5% front load this fund required. As I stated previously, I didn't think this front load would matter much given the high returns mutual funds were getting at this time. Then at year -end, they advertised how great this fund performed that past year. I clearly remember their saying the returns were 11.2%. Now you and I can do the math together. An 11.2% return on $10,000 should make my ending balance somewhere at $11,120. I then received my

statement in the mail several weeks later; the balance was somewhere like $9,750. This amount was less than my initial investment,
and yet the mutual fund "returned 11.2%" for the year.

Now, for clarity, I did not invest the $10,000 on January 1 of that year.
I think it was several months into it. I do remember the year did
not fluctuate much. But my experience clearly shows that the front
load and costs (expense ratio) passed along to me can and do lower
investment gains significantly. The shock of seeing my balance less
than the initial principal after a "return of 11.2%" was eye opening.

Invest in sector funds sparingly. They have a small place in any investment
portfolio. One sector in which I always have a position is the healthcare and
health-sciences industry.

[PMMWMMI] I have both T. Rowe Price Health Sciences and
Vanguard Health Care mutual funds. These sector funds are broadly
based in that they cover a wide spectrum of stocks that relate to
healthcare (hospitals, health insurance companies, health-related
products) and health sciences (biogenetics, research, medical product development). I view these two funds as index funds within a
sector fund. There are specialized and narrowly focused healthcare
and health-sciences sector funds, but the more narrow the fund's
focus, the riskier the fund.

I chose to invest in healthcare and health-sciences sector funds because I believe people will always get sick and will need healthcare.
As humans, we have a natural instinct to make our lives better and
live longer. The need for advances in health sciences will not abate.
This is one area in the economy where there will always be a demand.

[Main Point] My recommendation is to buy only no-load funds
and mostly index funds. They have the lowest expense ratios. Remember, mutual fund expenses are deducted every year. The higher

the expense ratio, the higher the return a fund must produce just to offset the costs and pass the leftover earnings to you.

ETFs

Exchange-traded funds are relatively new investment instruments. The popularity and accepted fact that index mutual funds outperform 80% of all actively managed funds is the genesis for ETFs.

Essentially, ETFs are hybrids of both stocks and mutual funds. They possess the diversity of mutual funds but buy and sell like stocks. They are also similar because they represent a collection of stocks with certain characteristic and objectives.

Unlike mutual funds, where orders to buy or sell are usually placed as a dollar amount (e.g., buy mutual fund ABC for $10,000), trades of ETFs are submitted like a stock for a number of shares at a particular price. Also unlike mutual funds, you can buy as little as one share of an ETF. Most mutual funds have a minimum purchase of several thousand dollars. The popular ones are as high as $50,000.

Since ETFs are bought and sold like stocks, there are brokerage fees. The good part about EFTs is that these fees are the same as for stocks. A $10,000 purchase on-line averages about $9 a trade. Mutual funds with loads are paid as a percentage of the purchase or the sale (if the load is back-end). Now let's look at what the cost would be with a typical load fund of 6% ($10,000 X .06 = $600). You can do the subtraction.

Also, unlike mutual funds, there are fewer expenses associated with EFTs. Although ETFs have expenses, they are much lower. As you recall from the previous section, mutual funds can have a wide range of fees such as broker commissions, front- or back-end loads, 12-b fees to market the fund, redemption fees, and many more.

Summary

There are many resources available that will rate and offer opinions about all the topics covered in this book so far. Many are free. You can always pay for a service that will make recommendations for stocks, mutual funds, and EFTs. For stocks, these services will include the suggested price and when to buy or sell. For mutual funds, the areas covered will be the experience of the fund manager, the primary objective of the fund, the index that the fund will be measured against to benchmark its performance, its performance over several periods, and many more important metrics of the fund.

The good news is that you have so much control. You do not have to do any studies or extensive research. With the internet, access to quality information and research are available with just a few clicks. The adage "Don't believe everything you read" now updates to "Don't believe everything you read on the internet," is still very true. You don't have to understand it all or even understand all the charts and statistics. Just ten to fifteen minutes a few times a week reading trusted articles from trusted sources about the stock market as a whole and about your specific stock will empower you with the knowledge to make sound investment choices.

[PMMWMMI] I subscribe to Zacks, Schaeffer's, and Analyst Ratings Network (ARN) free newsletters. I pay for subscriptions to The Motley Fool and Morningstar. (I am not endorsing these services, and I don't receive any compensation in any form from these businesses.)

CHAPTER THREE:
REGISTRATION TYPES

Before we discuss the tactics and strategies to increase our investment returns from the predictable patterns of the stock market, an understanding of the different types of registration accounts that hold our investment instruments is important.

> [Main Point] The location of certain investment instruments within a specific *tax* registration account type is important for our tactics for improved investment returns. As you will see in later chapters, the tactics will vary depending on the tax registration account type.

There are basically only three registration account types that hold investment instruments: taxable, tax-deferred, and tax-free.

Taxable; All Income/Gains Taxable.

Money placed into this registration type is from after-tax income. This means the money placed into this registration has already been taxed. Or put another way: any money placed into this registration type was not deducted on your tax return and did not lower your taxable income.

The original investment (principal) will not be taxed when sold or withdrawn. However, all income (interest and dividends) and realized gains (the difference between the value at sale minus the value you originally paid, also known as "cost basis") are taxable.

Any income or gains received in a calendar year will be taxed in that year regardless of whether you withdraw the money. Once you've reported any income or gains through the various 1099 forms you received for that tax year, they can be withdrawn with no tax ramifications.

> [Main Point] This should be the last registration type to place long -term investments. The maximum allowed should be placed into a 401(k) or an IRA (both are tax-deferred registration types) and a Roth IRA, an education ERA, or a 529 plan (these are tax-free withdrawal registration types) before any money is placed into this registration for long-term investment purposes.

Ordinary Income

Income and gains derived from investments held less than one year (short-term capital gain) are taxed as ordinary income. These income and gains are eventually lumped with income from wages and are taxed at the ordinary-income rate. The rate depends on your taxable income after deductions and other items that reduce taxable income. That rate can range from zero to as much as 39.6% in 2013. See Table 2-1.

Long-Term Capital Gains

Gains derived from investments held for one year or longer are taxed as a long -term capital gain. The maximum rate is 20% for those in the top tax bracket.

As explained previously in Chapter Two, the difference between ordinary income and long-term capital gain can be as much as 19.6% in taxes. That means the amount of gain for selling an investment held for less than one year will have to be 19.6% better than an investment held for one year just to break even. It is a stretch to justify buying a short-term investment that has to outperform a long-term investment by least 19.6%.

> **[Main Point]** The tax ramifications for investments held under this registration are too great to warrant using our tactics.

Tax-Deferred; Taxable at Withdrawal (401(k), IRA, SEP, Keogh)

Money placed into this registration type is from pre-tax income. This means the money placed into this registration has not been taxed. Or put another way: any money placed into this registration type was deducted on your tax return and lowered your taxable income. The principal placed in this registration will be taxed when withdrawn. There is a penalty of 10% if the money is withdrawn under certain conditions.

Any income or gains will not be taxed until withdrawn.

Since both principal and any earning are taxed when withdrawn and will have the same tax impact as ordinary-income rates, there is no distinction made at time of withdrawal.

Most people are familiar with this registration type. A typical company-sponsored 401(k) plan falls under this registration. Traditional IRAs also fall under this registration. Others are Keogh plans, SEP-IRAs, and Simple-IRAs. (These latter plans are for self-employed individuals and small businesses.)

Ordinary Income

All monies, both principal and gains, are taxed at ordinary-income rates when withdrawn. Since the tax deduction for the principal was taken (at the time taxes are filed), the U.S. Treasury wants back its taxes from the income that was deferred. That is why tax laws require distributions from these accounts no later than age 70 1/2. The mandatory withdrawals, called required minimum distributions (RMDs), can be delayed if the person is still earning wages. The amount required to be withdrawn is calculated using variables that are too complex to discuss here and has no bearing for our purposes.

> [Main Point] A tax-deferred registration is ideal for the tactics and strategy to be deployed because reallocating investments by selling and buying another investment *within* this registration, even between separate accounts under this same registration, will not incur penalties or taxes. (The movement of money between separate accounts must be done as a rollover or a transfer.)

Already Taxed; Tax-free at Withdrawal (Roth IRA, Coverdell Education IRA, 529 College Savings Plan)

Money placed into this registration type is from after-tax income. This means the money placed into this registration has already been taxed. Or put another way: any money placed into this registration was not deducted on your tax return and did not lower your taxable income.

No Taxable Income

Withdrawals are not taxed. Period. Both the original principal and any income or gains are not taxed at withdrawal.[3]

---

[3]There is a penalty of 10% if monies are withdrawn under certain conditions. Usually this occurs when monies are withdrawn before age 59 1/2 or on principal withdrawn within five years of the first principal contribution. If you opened a Roth IRA for tax year 2010 and made a contribution to it, all principal, including contributions made after 2010, can be withdrawn tax free after 2015.

There are no restrictions on how the money is used when withdrawn from a Roth IRA. There are restrictions on Coverdell Education IRAs and 529 College Savings accounts. The money withdrawn must be used for educational purposes. The allowable expenses are wide ranging and may include tuition, books, room and board, fees, computers, etc.

> **[PMMWMMI]** I had Coverdell Education IRAs for both my children. Paying no taxes on earnings is rare and is the best thing since sliced bread. In 2010, the provision to allow tax-free withdrawals for *any* educational purposes was about to expire. With the expiration of this provision, only secondary (college) educational expenses were allowed to be withdrawn tax free. I had to assess my life, and I accepted the fact that my special needs daughter will most likely not be able to attend college. So I had to withdraw all the money from her Education IRA to pay her educational needs (K-12) before the provision expired.
>
> Many investment companies that managed Coverdell Education IRAs stopped entirely. I had my children's Education IRAs at T. Rowe Price. They stopped opening new accounts. They allowed existing accounts to continue, but did not allow new money to be added.
>
> That provision allowing tax-free withdrawals for K-12 educational expenses was placed back into law with the signing of the American Taxpayer Relief Act on January 2, 2013.
>
> I opened new Coverdell Education IRA accounts for both my daughter and son at E-Trade and will roll over existing accounts from T. Rowe Price.

There is so much more when it comes to tax-deferred accounts and the tax implications associated with them that this book cannot discuss them all. Additionally, the reader's individual tax situation may be affected by these other restrictions. Always check with a qualified tax professional before acting on the tactics and strategies presented in this book.

[Main Point] The purpose of explaining these registration account types is to provide a basic understanding and set the table, if you will, for the upcoming tactics used in later chapters. The specific registration type plays a major role in our tactics and strategies to follow.

[PMMWMMI] I have investment instruments is all three tax registration account types.

CHAPTER FOUR:
ELECTRONIC TRADING AND ACCESS TO TIMELY INFORMATION

Buying and selling investment instruments has become very easy in the information age. Most employer 401(k) plans allow employees direct access to their accounts over internet connections. Changes can be made any time of the day or night and those instructions can be executed immediately or the next business day. Brokers and investment companies all allow access to accounts 24/7. Many allow the purchase and selling of multiple investment instruments (individual stocks, mutual funds, IRAs, ETFs, and many others) from within one account.

News and information about companies and their stock prices are available as soon as the articles are published on-line, and you can read all about them in your home at any time.

So, when you are ready to shift assets using the tactics and strategies in the next chapters, making changes to your portfolio will be quick and easy.

I have a cocktail party story to share with you. It's one of those stories of "what if . . .," "if I had done this . . . ," and "I could be a millionaire today if only. . . ."

Back in the late 1980s, when I was in my mid-20s, I liked science fiction as well as science in general. What fascinated me was how ideas, inventions, and science evolved from something simple, like a "Eureka" moment, to the final concept or invention that changed or helped humankind. Related to this, I have always looked for companies or emerging products that will make a big difference in our lives. Often these new products start with a simple idea that is refined until the products are useful and marketable.

I subscribed to a magazine called *Omni*. (It's no longer published.) This magazine was about science fiction and science. The central theme of the articles and stories was how the ideas within them affect human beings or humankind. In each issue of the magazine were two sections, one called "Matter" and the other called "Anti-Matter." The Matter section contained short articles or small news clips of up-and-coming research in science and medical science. The Anti-Matter section contained the same type of articles, but they were offbeat or weird in nature.

There was a short article in the Matter section that talked about a small British drug company called Burroughs Wellcome that was developing a new drug called AZT to fight the up-and-coming scourge of AIDS. I thought it would be a good investment to buy the stock of this company because the product had the potential to profoundly impact our lives and humanity.

I called my stockbroker and asked about this company and its stock. My broker said he had never heard of this company or the stock. I explained it was not a U.S. company. He said he would have to call down to another trading desk to find the information. (Now remember, this was the late 1980s. We had not entered the information age as yet. No internet, no Wi-Fi, no quick access to anything regarding the stock market.) My broker called back in about 45 minutes to my landline—no affordable cell phones back then either—and told me the price of the stock for that day was about 73 cents a share. Now, as a young, hot-blooded American male in his mid-20s with $2,000 burning a hole in his pocket and wanting to strike it rich, I wanted to buy this stock.

But all the sound investment rules and advice told me not to buy it. One common advice for that period was not to buy any stock if you could not track it closely. Again, this was the late 1980s where we got all stock prices in the back of the business section of the newspaper along with the other thousands of stock prices listed in small print from yesterday's closing. Another common advice for the individual stock investor was not to purchase foreign stocks. Again, one of the reasons for this is that it was even more difficult to track. The experience of my broker having to call another trading desk highlighted this very point about foreign stocks. Finally, since news took some time to reach the individual investor, especially research and development, it was difficult for me to track the development of the drug AZT along with any clinical trials and their results.

Based on all this standard and sound investment advice for that time, I, as a sound investor, followed this advice. I chose not to purchase the stock.

As we all know now, AZT has become one of the cornerstone drugs in the treatment of AIDS. The value of that company's stock has risen thousands of folds over the 73 cents a share that I was willing to pay. Through several mergers, Burroughs Wellcome is part of the pharmaceutical conglomerate Glaxo-SmithKline, ticker symbol (GSK) on the New York Stock Exchange.

This is a true story. But it's better left for telling during cocktail parties, especially with a drink in my hand.

[Main Point] Although following prevailing advice did not turn out well for me with Burroughs Wellcome, I've had substantial gains the vast majority of the time doing so. We cannot predict how future technology will change the way we invest. Follow current prevailing investment advice. Quality information about the company's stock price and any other information relating to the company are within easy reach. Read and learn, and make sound investment decisions.

CHAPTER FIVE:
STOCK MARKET PATTERNS

We finally come to our main thesis: the stock market is predictable because it moves in patterns driven by people's behavior based on their tendencies.

People are behind the movement of stocks.[4] Although many will say they decide to trade stocks based on specific reasons, the reasons are influenced by many underlying factors. Individual investors may have different reasons for their behavior than institutional investors. Institutional investors may have certain rules and constraints that they must operate under, but they too are people. Some of these tendencies are caused by tax laws, customs, traditions, policies and lifestyles. These tendencies create predictable patterns in the stock market. These predictable patterns can be exploited when we buy and sell. Remember our restaurant owner?

There have been uncountable theories, studies, and anecdotes explaining patterns in the stock market. Many are for short-term movements (within a month or even just one day). Others are for longer periods. Stock Trader's Almanac documents many of these patterns since the inception of the stock market. Some common patterns are called the "Santa Clause Rally," "Summer Rally," and the "January Effect." Other patterns are described using phrases such as "Wall Street's Free Lunch." and "Post-Presidential Year Syndrome."

---

[4]Yes, computer program trading is much more common and makes up 30% of all trades, based on July 2013 figures for the New York Stock Exchange. But it is people who program the software. It is people who decide which technical parameters the computer software will use to buy or sell at a particular price.

But purists do not believe patterns can emerge based on the "efficient-market" theory that everything that may influence the movement of the stock market will either cancel out or is already factored into the current state. This efficient-market theory just cannot be true. As explained in later chapters, there are many forces that affect investor behavior (individual, institutional, long-term, or active traders), which in turn affect stock market prices manifesting to discernable patterns in the stock market.

Our tactics to improve our returns uses two well-documented seasonal patterns within a long-term investment strategy. The first is described by the term "Halloween Effect." The second is described by the popular phrase, "Sell in May and go away."

There have been many studies that have shown that the stock market moves up and down in predictable seasonal patterns. They do not occur every year, but these patterns repeat themselves in 70–80% of the years. The patterns can be broken down into approximately two periods within a 12-month cycle. The first period starts in late fall until late spring (November to April)—the "Halloween Effect." The other period is between late spring through late fall (May to October)—"Sell in May and go away." For this book, we'll call the November-to-April time frame the Winter pattern and the May-to-October period the Summer pattern.

The Winter pattern shows stock prices gaining while the Summer pattern shows stock price staying flat or losing.

The often-cited 2002 study by Sven Bouman and Ben Jacobsen titled "The Halloween Indicator, 'Sell in May and Go Away': Another Puzzle" concluded:

> "Surprisingly, we find the Sell in May effect is present in 36 of the 37 countries in our sample. The effect tends to be particularly strong and highly significant in European countries, and also proves to be robust over time. Sample evidence shows that in a number of countries it has been noticeable for a very long time, and in the U.K.

stock market, for instance, we have found evidence of a Sell in May effect as far back as 1694. We find no evidence that the effect can be explained by factors like risk, cross correlation between markets, or the January effect. We also try some alternative explanations . . . but none of them seems to provide an explanation for the puzzle."

Sven Bouman and Ben Jacobsen. 2002. "The Halloween Indicator: 'Sell in May and Go Away': Another Puzzle." *American Economic Review*, 92(5): 1618-1635

Subsequent studies were conducted looking primarily at the U.S. stock market (as well as other countries) and essentially came to the same conclusion.

Still another study, conducted by Ben Jacobsen (same person cited above) and Nuttawat Visaltanachoti, both of Massey University in New Zealand, looked at the U.S. stock market specifically. Their conclusion was the same for the U.S. market:

"We find that the Halloween effect is related to different sectors. Consumer sectors tend to outperform during summer, while production sectors on average beat the market during winter. We find no link between summer and winter returns and liquidity measures, whether we consider the general market, or sector specific measures.

"The Halloween effect *proves to be a remarkable anomaly* [emphasis added]. As Schwert (2003) also points out, there are few anomalies that predict negative (*excess*) [emphasis added] returns as well as the Halloween effect. The negative returns are difficult to reconcile with time varying risk premiums or any equilibrium asset pricing model. The Halloween effect has *not weakened during the last decade* [emphasis added] and remains a puzzle for more than one reason."

Ben Jacobsen and Nuttawat Visaltanachoti, "The Halloween Effect in US Sectors." *The Financial Review*, 8 May 2006.

In a follow-up study, Ben Jacobsen and Cherry Yi Zhang (also from Massey University) looked at the Halloween effect for 108 counties. Their conclusion:

"This study investigates the Halloween effect for 108 countries over all the periods for which data is available.

"The Halloween effect is *prevailing around the world to the extent that mean returns are higher for the period of November–April than for May –October* [emphasis added] in 81 out of 108 countries, and the difference is statistically significant in 35 countries . . . having significantly higher May-October returns. Our evidence reveals that the size of the Halloween effect does vary cross-nation. It is stronger in developed and emerging markets than in frontier and rarely studied markets. Geographically, the Halloween effect is more prevalent in countries located in Europe, North America and Asia than in other areas. Subsample period analysis shows that the strongest Halloween effect among countries are observed in the past 50 years since 1960 and concentrated in developed Western European countries.

"The Halloween effect is still present out-of-sample in the 37 countries used in Bouman and Jacobsen (2002). The out-of-sample risk adjusted payoff from the Halloween trading strategy is still higher than for the buy and hold strategy in 36 of the 37 countries. When considering trading strategies assuming different investment horizons, the UK evidence reveals that investors with a long horizon would have remarkable odds of beating the market; with, for example, an investment horizon of 5 years, the chances that the Halloween strategy outperforms the buy and hold strategy is 80%, with the probability of beating the market increasing to 90% if we expand the investment horizon to 10 years.

"Overall, our evidence suggests that the Halloween effect is a *strong market anomaly that has strengthened rather than weakened* [emphasis added] in the recent years. Plausible explanations of the Halloween effect should be able to allow for time variation in the effect and explain why the effect has strengthened in the last 50 years."

Ben Jacobsen and Cherry Yi Zhang. "The Halloween Indicator: Everywhere and All the Time." Social Science Research Network, 1 Oct. 2012.

In 2010, K. Stephan Haggard and H. Douglas Witte, both from Missouri State University, researched whether there was seasonality to the U.S. stock market and confirmed its existence. Their conclusion:

"In this study, we show that the *Halloween effect in U.S. returns is significant in the period 1954–2008* [emphasis added], but not before. Anomalies usually are present only in older data, given that they can be exploited for profit by savvy investors once they are identified. This does not appear to be the case with the Halloween effect. We also show that the Halloween effect is robust to consideration of outliers, the January effect, and transactions costs. Some anomalies, such as those related to weather, would require many transactions per year and a touch of clairvoyance to exploit, making profitability from exploitation of these anomalies questionable. By contrast, the *Halloween effect is an especially attractive anomaly for investors* [emphasis added], given the low number of transactions required and the easily predictable dates of those transactions. The greater risk -adjusted returns available by *investing in a Halloween portfolio are a challenge to the efficient markets hypothesis* [emphasis added]. Further research is needed to reconcile these results with rational human behavior."

K. Stephan Haggard and H. Douglas Witte. 2010. "Halloween Effect: Trick or Treat?" *International Review of Financial Analysis.* 19(5).

In June 2013, an article by Jeffrey Hirsch in *American Association of Individual Investors* (AAII) cited the following graph (Figure 5-1) from Stock Trader's Almanac showing the average percentage of returns in each calendar month. Five of the best six months fall within our Winter pattern, and five of the six worst months fall within our Summer pattern. This empirical data confirms the academic studies.

Figure 5-1. DJIA Monthly Annual Percentage Gain (1950–2012)

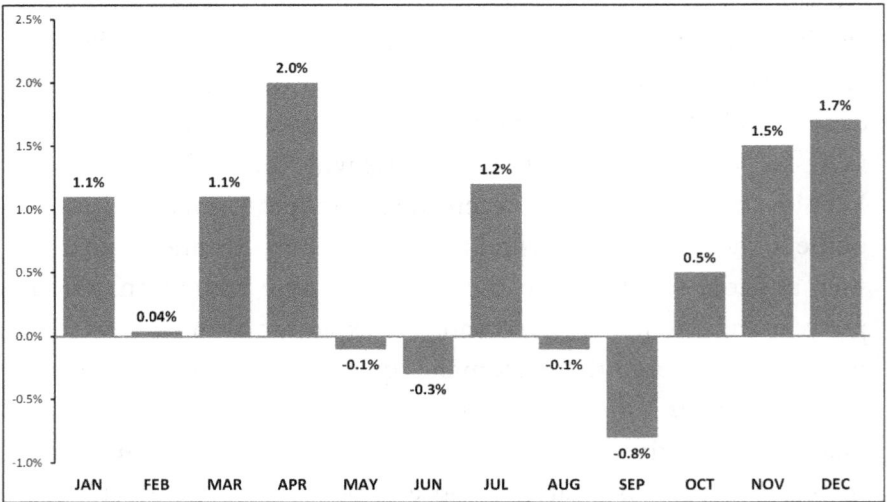

Source: Adapted from Stock Trader's Almanac. Cited in Jeffrey Hirsch, "Using Seasonal and Cyclical Stock Market Patterns." *AAII* Journal, June 2013. Posted on aaii.com January 19, 2014.

Figure 5-2 shows the rate of change in the Dow Jones Industrial Index in the best six months (which includes July, the only month within the Summer pattern). The difference between the best and worst six months is 7.2%. That is a significant difference.

Figure 5-2. Average Percentage Change in DJIA Since 1950

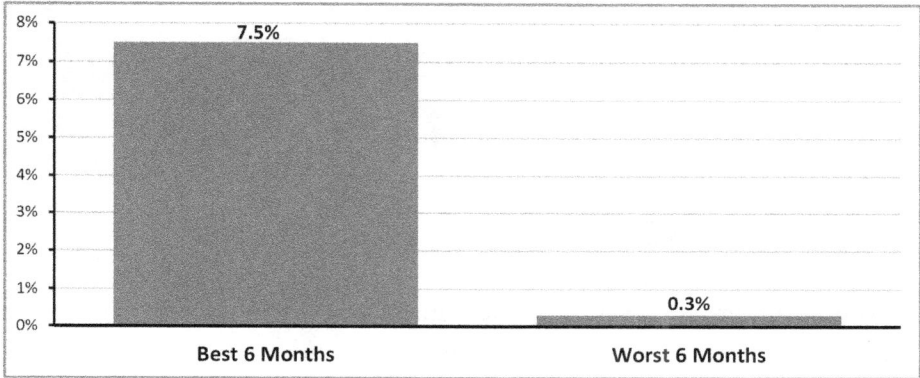

Source: *Adapted from Stock Trader's Almanac.* Cited in Jeffrey Hirsch. June 2013.
"Using Seasonal and Cyclical Stock Market Patterns". *AAII Journal.*
Posted on aaii.com January 19, 2014.

The studies cited, along with 100 years of historical hard data compiled by Stock Trader's Almanac, show the stock market is not efficient. The stock market is not an independent self-monitoring organism at equilibrium. Its seasonal patterns of movement up and down are predictable a vast majority of the time. The evidence is compelling.

Chapter Six:
Forces Creating Patterns

Why do the two seasonal patterns behave differently?

Does the Summer pattern reflect the anomaly of losses or being mostly flat? Or does the Summer pattern reflect a normal trend, and the Winter pattern is the anomaly of higher returns? What forces will cause these two periods to have such different stock market patterns and the investor behavior they reflect?

Taxes and Contributions to Retirement Accounts

There has been a fundamental shift in retirement funding during the past 30 years. There are many fewer defined benefit pension plans and significantly more self-funded retirement plans such as 401(k)'s and IRAs. It's the new normal.

Contributions to retirement accounts are the dominant effect on the Winter pattern. As noted previously, the Winter pattern is becoming more pronounced. The increasing popularity and necessity of self-funded retirement accounts is the single driving force as to why the Winter pattern is strengthening in prominence.

The statutory deadline of April 15 for the last day of contributions of the tax year is a major contributing factor. This is the time when individuals focus away from other life matters into taxes and adding to their retirement accounts

Individuals who have additional money to invest often add that cash to the stock market between January and April before the deadline to contribute of April 15. During this period, contributions can be made for the previous tax year (if no contribution was made for that year) along with the current tax year.

Small businesses tend to fund their employer matches at this time of the year. If there is some latitude to how much they contribute, businesses wait until they have estimated their tax obligations before making decisions on how much they are willing to contribute. Businesses that are on a calendar-year basis, which are the majority, will not know their tax obligations until this time of the year.

Smaller businesses that contribute to SEPs and Simple IRAs operate under these same conditions. Businesses of this size do not fund retirement accounts until their taxes are nearly complete. That's because they can decide whether to contribute from 0% up to 25% of compensation. For the owners under a pass-through business such as an "S" corporation, a limited liability company (LLC), partnerships, or a sole proprietorship, the compensation in most cases is the net income for the year. But they don't know what that income is until late into the tax season. They wait to fund contributions for both owner and employees, adding to the influx of cash to be invested in the stock market in March or April.

When there is an influx of cash entering the market, the demand for equities tends to drive up stock prices. Those who wish to purchase individual stocks are more willing to pay a higher price to move from cash to equities. Fund managers must buy stocks even if they think the stocks in a fund are already overpriced because he or she has no choice unless the fund's prospectus allows for a large cash position.

Let's revisit Figure 5-1 showing the average return by month. We see a big up -tick in March and then a spike in April. April has the highest rate of return for any month of the year.

Fund Distribution Policies

Other than income-producing mutual funds, which distribute income or gains monthly or quarterly, most mutual funds distribute dividends and capital gains near the end of the calendar year, usually in the month of December.

There is some stabilizing force to the market caused by the general policy that any gains from the mutual fund are distributed in the month of December. This policy affects investor behavior. It is generally unwise to sell mutual funds at this time of the year and miss out on receiving any gains or potential write -offs in losses. Those who own the fund at the date of record [5] as declared by the mutual fund will receive those gains.

If you sold before that date, you will not receive those distributions even if you held it for most of the calendar year. You still benefited from the increase of the NAV value if you were to sell the fund, but you will miss out on any gains for the year. It's like quitting your job just before the Christmas bonus. Unless there are good reasons, most informed investors do not sell in the months leading to distributions.

Institutional Investors' Incentives and Obligations

Institutional Investors' Self-Interest

Most institutional investors [6] tend to be underinvested toward the latter part of the year. They want to have an adequate supply of cash to make investment

---

[5] The date of record is an arbitrary date that is used to determine which investors (those listed as owning shares according to company records) will receive dividends.

[6] Institutional investors are those who manage mutual funds, pensions, and hedge funds.

moves to react to what the market is doing or has done during the year. But individual investors live their lives around the calendar year, and they will be looking closely at their year-end statements. Institutional investors are under pressure to be fully or almost fully invested for the calendar year. They tend to do more buying during the latter part of the year. This affects their behavior by their willingness to bid up stock prices to get out of the cash positions and not be underinvested.

Since most institutional investors have a tendency to manage the assets this way, there is pressure to outperform their peers, who are also driving up prices. This competition tends to feed off each other in the form of higher stock prices.

There is also the strategy of fund managers' selling stocks in December that have done poorly to take losses and thus deductions in the current tax year and then repurchase stock after the new year. This may offset part of the buying spree, but it is offset by taking the cash from selling at a loss and reinvesting the same cash in January. Each part, selling at year-end then buying back in the new year, may have purposeful tax implications for the institutional investor who does this, but the net effect tends to cancel out within the entire market. It doesn't matter for our purpose because it's a short term gyration within the overall Winter pattern of greater stock returns.

Institutional Investors' Obligations

Most employee bonuses are paid during the month of December, including those of institutional fund managers. With this added money concentrated in this part of the calendar, more money is used for spending. Some of that money will be invested in the stock market, creating more cash which then requires fund managers to buy more stock and push prices up further.

Although pension fund and hedge fund managers generally have more latitude on when to invest any cash influx, mutual fund managers generally must buy when investors send in money. As mentioned earlier, a manager may not want to buy more because stocks are overpriced. But the prospectus may limit the proportion of cash that is allowed in the fund. He then has to purchase stocks, usually at overvalued prices. The manager will buy in total disregard to fundamentals or valuation; he'll buy simply because he must.

Do fund managers eat their own cooking?

There is some pressure for fund managers to put their own money in the same mutual fund they manage. Some firms strongly encourage their managers to so because this demonstrates stewardship and is a great marketing tool. It is a strong selling point for the fund family to say the interests of both the manager and the investor are the same.

That a fund manager has her own money in the fund she manages is so important, Morningstar (a company that specializes in rating mutual funds) includes this as a variable in determining the rating of stewardship it assigns to each fund. It's a high probability that a portion of bonuses the manager received is reinvested in the market, helping prices to rise in the Winter pattern.

If the fund manager doesn't eat her own cooking, she most likely will at least eat in the same restaurant.

As an investor, you believe the stock market is one of the best places to place your money. That's why you are reading this book. Fund managers work within the stock market and know how profitable it is to invest in equities. It's safe to say they place a portion of their surplus year-end bonuses back into equities. This additional flow of money is another reason for stock prices to go higher during the Winter pattern.

Investor Psychology

People have a tendency to fund their retirement accounts late into the tax season, creating a pattern of increased funds to the market and driving stock prices. As mentioned above, fund managers must buy stocks even if they think the stocks in their portfolio are already overpriced.

Investors have legitimate reasons for waiting until January to April of the next year to fund their IRAs because some may have to wait to see if they meet or are restricted from contributing based on their tax situation.

> [PMMWMMI] I've jumped the gun a few times and made contributions to my SEP IRA thinking I was prudent to fund the account before my tax situation has been finalized. I ended up having less income or wages than I originally thought. I had to correct my "excess contributions" by withdrawing all that money from the SEP account (deferred tax registration) and placing it in a regular investment account (taxable registration) for the same tax year with no penalty. If I didn't withdraw the excess by my filing date or April 15, a 6% penalty would have been assessed.
>
> I paid for my mistake, literally. Although I transferred the stocks into a taxable registration and did not actually sell them, the gain was nonetheless treated as ordinary income per IRS rules. Ouch.
>
> Two good things can be derived from this. Since I paid taxes, I must have made money. There is nothing wrong with making money even if I have to pay some taxes on it. The second is that I still exercised good investment practice by funding my IRAs soon into the tax season for that tax year instead of waiting until the following spring (between January and April of the next calendar year).

However, the primary reason for waiting until the next year is laziness. I've been guilty of it myself.

According to the Vanguard Group study conducted on their customers from 2007 through 2012, 41% of traditional IRA and Roth IRA contributions were made between January and April of the following year. And of that 41%, half of that was invested in the first two weeks of April alone. Wow, talk about cutting it close.

The study found that only about 10% was invested in the month of January of the same tax year. As explained above, there are legitimate reasons to wait until the following calendar year until the tax ramifications are clear before putting money into retirement accounts. But for the majority of investors, there are no reasons but procrastination. Exercise good investing practices. Put some money into retirement accounts as soon as possible and then fund the balance when your tax situation is known.

> [PMMWMMI] In my SEP IRA explanation above, the amount I could fund was conditional on my final tax situation. But there are other accounts that have little to do with the final tax calculations. I fund my children's Coverdell Education IRAs within the first week of the new tax year. I also do the same for my Roth IRA. Since these two accounts start earning money tax free, it makes no sense to have that money sit either in a savings account or in stocks, earning money that will be taxed until I move it later in the year.

There are no tax laws that significantly influence mass investor behavior during the months within the Summer pattern. Although businesses that are on a fiscal-year basis may end during the Summer pattern and have to deal with tax consequences, there are many other companies that are on a fiscal-year basis whose year-end is spread out among the other months of the calendar. There is no concentration of tax effects, unlike those in December through April.

Investor indifference in the Summer pattern is a major factor. One often-repeated theory for this behavior is that investors are off vacationing or at least are thinking about it. Investors are in more of a relaxed mood and tend to avoid matters that may cause stress, such as researching a company and its stock.

Additionally, during the summer months when children are out of school, parents are more focused on providing activities for their children and organizing the work week around them.

I also suspect that money is of a shorter supply at this time of the year. As with most investors, much of the investment money has already been placed in retirement accounts just a few months ago near the tax-filing deadline. Vacations cost money and require additional expenditures beyond the typical monthly expenses. These cut into any money that potentially may be placed into investments.

At the beginning of this chapter, I posed the questions: Does the Summer pattern reflect the anomaly of losses or being mostly flat? Or does the Summer pattern reflect a normal trend, and the Winter pattern is the anomaly of higher returns?

I say the Summer pattern is typical of the stock market relative to investor behavior. There is really nothing going on during this time of the year relating to taxes or any calendar milestones for fund managers except the quarter-ending statements for June and September. Although they have an interest to show positive quarter-end results on their clients' statements, they know the primary focus will be on the year-end statement in December.

Why is September negative historically?

As Figure 5-1 from the previous chapter shows, September is the single worst month with an average negative return of 0.8%. It is worse than the second-worst month (June) by a large difference of 0.5%

My theory: to pay for school or college. Although it would be smart to transition out of equities and into safer instruments four or five years before the money is needed, most people keep their money in equities until the last minute.

Also, redemptions from investments for lingering expenses from the vacation months add to September's average negative returns.

CHAPTER SEVEN:
THE TACTICS WITHIN SOUND
INVESTMENT STRATEGIES

General Approach

We finally get to the tactics we will use to exploit the predictable patterns of the stock market.

Tactic 1: Move money out of investment instruments that have a *high* correlation to the movement of the entire stock market. Move that same money into investment instruments that have a *low* correlation or no correlation to the movement of the entire stock market. We do this between mid-April and mid-May near the end of the Winter pattern.

Tactic 2: Move money out of investment instruments that have a *low* correlation or no correlation to the movement of the entire stock market. Move that same money into investment instruments that have a *high* correlation to the movement of the entire stock market. We do this between mid-October and mid-November near the end of the Summer pattern. (Yes, this is the exact opposite of *Tactic 1*.)

Tactic 3: Any money received and designated for investment in the stock market (stocks, mutual funds, ETFs) during the Summer pattern will be placed only in investment instruments that have a *low* correlation or no correlation to the movement of the entire stock market. When the Winter pattern arrives, execute *Tactic 2*.

Tactic 4: Any money received and designated for investment in the stock market during the Winter pattern will be placed only in investment instruments that have a *high* correlation to the movement of the entire stock market. When the Summer pattern arrives, execute *Tactic 1*.

Types of Investment Instruments

High Correlation to the Movement of the Entire Stock Market

High-correlation investment instruments move up or down with the overall movements of the stock market. Some examples are:

- Index funds
- ETFs
- Most mutual funds (except narrowly defined sector funds)
- Most foreign mutual funds (except narrowly defined foreign funds)
- Most individual stocks

Some sector or foreign funds, however, are so narrowly defined in terms of what and where the fund can invest that these funds will move up or down on factors unique to that sector or that part of the world only, and not with the broader stock market.

Low Correlation or No Correlation to the Movement of the Entire Stock Market

Low-correlation investment instruments move up or down on their own unique factors and less with the overall movement of the stock market. Examples are:

- Savings accounts
- CD's (certificates of deposit)
- Money market accounts and funds
- Commercial paper
- Short-term bond funds
- Income-producing mutual funds
- Narrowly defined sector mutual funds
- Narrowly defined foreign mutual funds
- Stable income funds
- Municipal bond funds
- Defensive stock mutual funds
- Dividend-yielding mutual funds
- Defensive stocks

Defensive stocks are from companies that tend to be large and well established. These are utilities, energy firms, and consumer-staples companies that have a tendency to have stable stock prices because the demand for their products does not fluctuate with economic trends. Similar to defensive stocks, stocks (or funds) that pay dividends are from large and well-established companies. Most large and established companies pay dividends on their stocks; most young and growth-oriented companies need the money from earnings to expand and therefore seldom pay dividends.

> [Main Point] Once you've established one to three low-correlation instruments that fit your risk tolerance, all you have to do is decide which years to use these tactics and what percentage of your portfolio to shift. And if you are already satisfied with your high -correlation instruments, just shift the money back to them. You don't have to do additional research into newer ones.

Reallocating out of equities and into cash-based accounts or income-producing accounts may seem ill-advised during times when interest rates are low, as is the current environment. But a small positive return is still better than a negative return. The tactics will be more effective when interest rates for these types of investments are back to their historical averages of around 6%. See Table 7-1. The low interest rates we are currently experiencing are not the norm.

Table 7-1. Federal Reserve Interest Rates

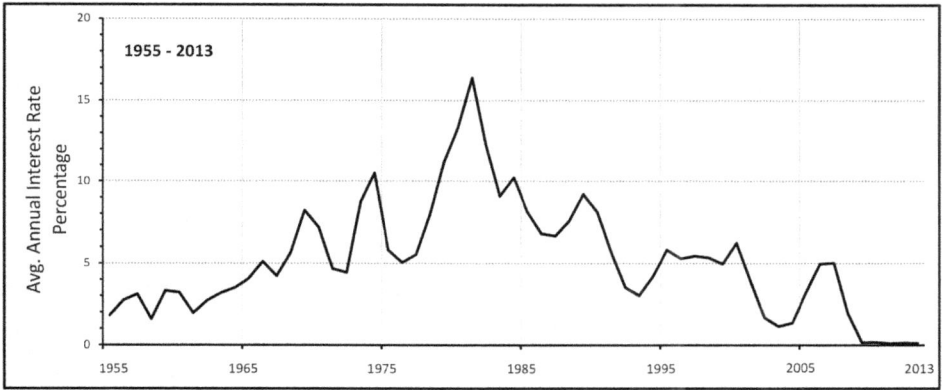

Source: Adapted from TradingEconomics.com.

Double Your Money

There is a universally accepted formula called the "72 rule" to estimate how many years it would take to double your money. The unknown is the average rate of return of that money. In any investment timeframe, it is very difficult to get a constant rate of return over several years. Still, the 72 rule gives us a good estimate.

The formula is to simply divide 72 by the whole number of the estimated rate of return. For instance, assuming a constant rate of return of 5%, the formula would be 72/5 = 14.4. In other words, if you can get a constant return of 5%, you'll double your money in about 14.4 years. See Table 7-2.

Table 7-2. Double Your Money – "72 Rule"

Annual Growth Rate	Years to Double	Annual Growth Rate	Years to Double	Annual Growth Rate	Years to Double
1%	72.0	6%	12.0	11%	6.5
2%	36.0	7%	10.3	12%	6.0
3%	24.0	8%	9.0	13%	5.5
4%	18.0	9%	8.0	14%	5.1
5%	14.4	10%	7.2	15%	4.8

Source: Adapted from Mohindra, Amit. "The Rule of 72."
The Nelson Touch Blog, 28 Feb. 2011.

Let's apply this method to the difference of investing in the best six months versus the worst six months of the year. As noted in Chapter Five, in Figure 5-2, the best (7.5%) minus the worst (0.3%) yields a difference of 7.2%. We'll round down to an even 7%. Using the formula of the "72 rule," 72/7 = 10.3. That means you'll double your investments with just our tactics alone over a ten-year span. This doesn't include the additional gains from the investments themselves over the ten years.

I understand our example above includes the month of July, so the actual difference is less than 7.2%. There are other considerations that may change the actual timeframe. But the example illustrates the power of these investment tactics within a long-term strategy.

Primer

Before we apply the above tactics to actual investment instruments, let talk about what the tactics will and will not do, along with some caveats.

These tactics are for long-term investors incorporating the buy-and-hold strategy. But "buy-and-hold" does not mean buy-and-ignore. As a long-term investor, you know you can't time the market. True, but you can shift invest-ments around to exploit documented and proven patterns of the stock market. Having the opportunity to gain positive returns 70–80% of the time are amaz-ing percentages when it comes to the stock market. Note that I am not saying you'll receive 70–80% returns; I am saying positive returns on your investment 70–80% of the time. Even if the investments return an average of 3–5% for 70–80% of the time, this is a financial windfall for doing nothing but shifting assets to different investment instruments at the right time of the year within each pattern.

These tactics do not indiscriminately sell equities. These tactics do not indis-criminately buy equities. I am not suggesting that we dump all stocks, mutual funds, and ETFs and then put all the money into cash.

Stocks

These tactics do not focus on selling individual stocks. In fact, with a few exceptions, individual stocks are not part of the tactics we will deploy. There have to be compelling reasons to sell a specific stock. The fundamental reasons you bought that stock in the first place must no longer exist to warrant selling that particular stock. I do not recommend using the tactics for individual stocks, especially if they are in a taxable registration.

No-Load Mutual Funds

The best investment instrument for exercising this strategy is no-load mutual funds. There are no costs to buy the fund and no cost to exit the fund.[7] Some no-load fund managers impose a small penalty (also called "redemption fees") They are usually 1–2% of the amount repurchased within a period of time to

---

[7]Technically there is a very small cost. Every transaction within any mutual fund will incur some trading cost. The costs are allocated to *all* fund holders, usually near the end of the calendar year, in the form of an adjustment to the NAV of the fund.

discourage constant buying and selling. The typical periods are one to three months. Some mutual funds impose a waiting period of up to one year.

Mutual funds generally use a "first in first out" (FIFO) basis to determine if redemption fees apply. As an example, let's say you already have $10,000 in the fund, and you recently put in another $2,000. But within the redemption penalty period for the additional monies, you decide to take out $5,000. The mutual fund will look at the redemption of $5,000 as coming from the $10,000 that was already there. They will not treat the recently added $2,000 as part of the $5,000 taken out. In this case, no redemption fees are charged.

Some funds do not allow any purchases within a certain period after a distribution.

Check with your mutual fund for any of these restrictions.

These restrictions should not be an issue because our tactics are deployed in approximately six-month intervals.

Load Mutual Funds

Load mutual funds add a dimension of additional cost to our tactics. Whether you should apply our tactics to load mutual funds depends heavily on whether the sale from one mutual fund can have the load waived by the receiving mutual fund. In some cases, those loads on the purchased fund will be waived if both funds are from the same family of funds. That's not a guarantee, though. Check with the mutual fund company to ask about "NAV transfers." If you have to pay the loads just selling and then buying the same amount between funds for the purpose of executing our tactics, then I would suggest you do not do it. Unless the load is a fraction of a percentage point, the cost of the load would offset too much of the potential gains of our tactics.

ETFs

The tactics for ETFs are basically the same as for no-load mutual funds. ETFs do not have loads, and there are no restriction periods or redemption penalties. They offer more flexibility for us to use the tactics than mutual funds. However, there are brokerage fees to buy and sell ETFs just like stocks. Brokerage fees are generally very small and the cost to buy once a year and sell once a year (even for each ETF) will not have much of an impact on our returns using our tactics.

A Note of Caution

If any of your investments are managed by a third party, check to see if there are additional transaction or management fees to sell and buy beyond the typical brokerage fee for ETFs and stocks. If there are, you'll have to weigh those costs against the potential gains using our tactics.

> [Main Point] Don't sell everything. Sell only those investment instruments that have a high correlation to the movement of the whole stock market, and keep the rest where they are. The combination of all instruments using the tactics will be only a portion of your portfolio. But that portion has the potential to have a higher gain or less of a loss than if you left it to move with the general market.
>
> These few percentage gains will add up to a lot over years of investing. Statistics show that even a few extra percentage-point gains over the long term will amount to large gains in the future.

Reallocation/Rebalancing

These tactics of shifting assets are consistent with sound investment practices.

Sound investment practice is to rebalance your portfolio or mix of investments at least once a year to match your investment goals. Your investment goals should include a set percentage of the various assets you want to own based on your risk level. When these proportions are not where you want them to be, then shift assets back to the proportions that are comfortable for you. Rebalancing is also the time to reevaluate poorly performing investments and determine if you should sell them.

Our tactic of shifting assets between seasonal patterns is the best time to do something that we should do anyways: rebalance.

Let's look at the end of the Winter pattern, for example. We rebalance our portfolio by selling some high-correlation investment instruments. But instead of putting the money back into high-correlation instruments, we place them into low correlation instruments as our tactics say to do. Taking some money off the table is part of a sound investing tactic called a "defensive" move.

We take some extra time during the Summer pattern to research and decide which high-correlation investments to buy back at the end of the Summer pattern. When we do, we've completed the cycle of rebalancing our portfolio.

Remember, we are not doing this for all of your investment instruments, only those explained above. Most of our other investments will continue to be fully invested in equities.

What If the Stock Market Goes Up during the Summer Pattern?

If stock market returns are higher than our safer investments during the Summer pattern, the only negative is that we've lost opportunity gains. This is a legitimate concern when making investment decisions. We don't want to be left behind. But losing potential gains is better than losing real money. We manage our money to maximize earnings and minimize losses. Remember, we are shifting money out of high-correlation investments because the Summer pattern has a high chance of losses.

Investing is not gambling. Gambling is being willing to accept the chances that the investment can lose 50% while having the chance to win 50%. Investing is about capital preservation. Investing is maximizing returns while safeguarding against loss—great financial loss. Proper investing attitude acknowledges that you can afford to gain 50% *but cannot* afford to lose 50%. Let's use an example. We invest $10,000. We can invest in an instrument that might return $5,000 or lose $5,000. Or we can invest in an instrument that might return $700 or lose $700. If you are a gambler, then you would choose the $5,000 win-or-lose investment. But as an investor, you would choose the $700 win-or-lose investment because you cannot afford to lose $5,000 even though you know you could gain $5,000.

Investing will not garner large returns in short periods. Equity investments returning an average of 7–10% over a period of time are considered good for the stock market. The reason is that, historically, that's the average return over time in the stock market. It's a fact that the market goes up over time, but slowly. Investing is taking a small risk to earn a small but reasonable gain over time.

When to Execute the Tactics

When is the exact moment to execute this strategy? The tactics should be used mid-April to mid-May and again mid-October to mid-November. Do the research and get a sense of how the economy is moving. See how businesses are performing and what direction the stock market is headed. Listen to and evaluate what trusted authors and articles are saying; listen to yourself. These tactics should be considered every year. But get a sense of whether you should use the tactics *this* year, and when. There is no empirical number through some fancy calculation of matrixes to pop up and say "Go" or "No." If you've been doing your homework and educating yourself, you'll gain a sense and understanding of the dynamics of how the stock market moves. Your gut is good enough, and it will be right most of the time.

Strategy for Each Registration Type

Taxable

Since this registration type is taxable, any sale is subject to tax ramifications in the same calendar year. This means that money from another source or a portion of the gain will be used to pay the tax. This clearly cuts into the amount you actually made and the money to pay taxes will no longer continue to work for you. Unless you feel strongly that an individual stock, ETF, or mutual funds will gain significantly more to warrant the risk and tax ramifications, I do not recommend using the tactics for investments in this registration type. Whether you've held the investment for under a year (ordinary-income tax rate) or over a year (the lower, capital gains tax rate) does not matter as the tax consequences are too high to use the tactics.

Tax Deferred; Taxable at Withdrawal (401(k), IRA, SEP, Keogh) and Tax-Free at Withdrawal (Roth IRA, Coverdell Education IRA, 529 College Savings Plan)

These registration types are perfect for our tactics.

> [Main Point] There are a few subtle differences between these two registrations types, but for our purposes, the effects of the tactics on each are the same. So we'll combine them, and the following discussions apply to each.

Since there are no immediate tax ramifications, the tactics will work very well for investments in these registration types. Unlike taxable registrations, monies to pay for taxes stay in the account and will continue to earn money.

There may be some costs that will be incurred. Stocks and ETFs will incur brokerage fees. As discussed previously, mutual funds with loads (both front

-end and back-end) may incur a cost. And if your investments are managed by a third party, there may be some additional transactional costs. Any costs must be weighed against the potential gains of using the tactics.

Use our tactics within your 401(k) plan. Choose a money market or fixed-income type of instrument and shift the money into one of these accounts. Or shift the money into any of the other low or no-correlation instruments list above if offered within your plan. Confirm there is no fee for selling an instrument and buying another. Most 401(k) plans allow reallocating your investments without a fee. Some plans limit the number of times that can be done within a set period.

The same applies to IRAs of any type.

Within these registrations, we can be a little more aggressive with individual stocks. Since gains from their sale do not trigger taxes, we have some liberty. Use the tactics only on stable large companies that have a high correlation to the movement of stocks. The only other situation where individual stocks are sold is when the fundamentals don't apply any more to make you believe that the stock price will continue to increase over time. Do this sparingly, as each trade will incur small brokerage fees.

If you have a large mutual fund, then I recommend selling in one-quarter increments. If you think the market will decrease slightly during the Summer pattern, then sell only one-quarter of the fund. If you think the market will fall more, than sell a larger portion of one-half to maybe three-quarters. But do not sell all, and do not close the fund. Some funds may be "closed," meaning they will not allow new accounts for that fund. If you closed the fund, you may not be able to get back into the fund.

As a hedge, you should always keep a portion of a fund just in case the market goes higher, so you can still participate in it. Additionally, some mutual funds have a minimum-balance requirement and may impose an administrative fee for going below it. Minimum-balance fees may be waived if the aggregate household investments exceed a threshold amount. Check with the fund.

[PMMWMMI] I own mutual funds in only three families. Vanguard, T. Rowe Price, and Fidelity all have aggregate household thresholds that, when reached, eliminate low-balance or other administrative fees.

As explained earlier, the load cost may be prohibitive to execute the tactics with load mutual funds. However, you can still participate with us by buying no-load funds going forward. Then use the tactics on the new no-load funds in future cycles.

Summary of Tactics

- The tactics should be considered every year.
- Break out the stock market seasonal patterns into the Winter pattern and the Summer pattern.
- The Winter pattern is from November to April, which includes the five best-performing months; and the Summer pattern is from May to October, which includes the five worst-performing months.
- Use the tactics near the end or beginning of each seasonal pattern.
- The transition from the Winter pattern to the Summer pattern is when you sell a portion of your portfolio of high-correlation investment instrument and place that money into low- or no-correlation investment instruments.
- The transition from the Summer pattern to the Winter pattern is when you sell a portion of your portfolio of low or no-correlation investment instruments and use that money to buy high-correlation investment instruments.
- Any additional money available to invest in equities during the first four months of Winter pattern should be used to purchase high-correlation instruments. Monies available during the last two months of the Winter pattern should be placed in low or no-correlation instruments. We do

not invest in high-correlation instruments the last two months because the holding period is too short.

- Any additional money available to invest in equities during all months of Summer pattern should be used to purchase low or no-correlation instruments.
- Unless a stock no longer meets the fundamental reasons that the stock was originally purchased, do not sell any individual stocks using these tactics in taxable registrations. Sell and buy stocks sparingly within tax-deferred registrations.
- Reallocate only a portion of no-load index funds and no-load mutual funds using 25% increments.
- Reallocate only a portion of ETFs using 25% increments.
- Do not reallocate mutual funds that charge loads—unless an NAV transfer is offered by the fund.
- Do not reallocate no-load mutual funds that will incur redemption fees.

There you have it. Put that extra effort into managing your investments. These tactics do not take much work on your part. It's done only twice a year. You will find that little extra effort will make a big difference in your wealth over the long term. Happy investing for your future and your family's future.

My Purpose in Writing This Book

The primary purpose of writing this book is to share my personal knowledge and experience navigating through the seemingly endless complexities of the stock market. Although we hear about the stock market every day and as of 2011, 54% of all Americans own some stocks in one form or another (mostly through our retirement accounts and pensions), it's still an enigma for the vast majority of us.

I've tried to filter and summarize the complexities regarding taxes, regulations, investing practices, and investment instruments to provide you the basic important issues that only really matter for us—the busy, everyday, long-term, individual investor hoping to make a better future for ourselves and our family. I hope I was successful in writing about these topics with clarity and brevity.

I encourage you to make that little extra effort to read and learn what you can, given the demands of your busy life. It really doesn't take much time out of your week. Do this over a short period, and you'll quickly know and understand the factors that affect the patterns in the stock market. With that knowledge, you will become a confident investor controlling your own path to future wealth.

WHAT LAWYERS SAY I MUST SAY

Although I have the background, both academically and through personal experience, to write this book, this book expresses my knowledge and opinions only. Investing is not empirical. It is not a science. It is an intellectual process of understanding and educating ourselves about sound investment principles to make the best investment decisions to which we are capable.

The opinions and tactics described in this book are well documented and are used effectively by many investors. But there is no guarantee they will work for you. You already know that. Right? But we live our lives every day based on the chances of something happening or not happening. In my opinion, using the tactics described in this book will increase your chances of higher investment returns than just riding along with the stock market in general.

I am not offering investment advice to trade any of the stocks, mutual funds, ETFs, or any other investments mentioned in this book. I also do not have any financial interest in any of the investment instruments mention beyond my personal interest to see these investments grow for my future and that of my children.

ABOUT THE AUTHOR

Francis H. Yee has a Bachelor in Business Administration with a major in Finance. He has always been interested in the stock market and how it behaves. He bought his first stocks in a private business at age 15 and made his first public stock trade at 23.

As the dad of two children, he's made saving money and investing for them a high priority. Over many years of investing, he has made some wise choices and he's made many mistakes. But he's learned from both. Mr. Yee's observations and experience give him the insight to stock market patterns and the investor behaviors that create them.

He has exploited those observations and developed investment tactics within a fundamentally sound long-term investment strategy.

References and Resources

Preface

"Exchange-Traded Fund—ETF." *Investopedia.com.* Investopedia, n.d. Web. 2 Feb. 2014.
http://www.investopedia.com/terms/e/etf.asp

Fuhrmann, Ryan. "How Has the Stock Market Changed?" *Investopedia.com.* Investopedia, 10 Nov. 2011. Web. 6 Jan. 2014.
http://www.investopedia.com/financial-edge/1111/how-has-the-stock-market-changed.aspx

Johnston, Michael. "Brief History of ETFs." *Finance.yahoo.com.* Yahoo, 11 Sept. 2012. Web. 24 Jan. 2014.
http://finance.yahoo.com/news/brief-history-etfs-130054577.html

McWhinney, James. "A Brief History of the Mutual Fund." *Investopedia.com.* Investopedia, 7 Sept. 2009. Web. 7 Jan. 2014.
http://www.investopedia.com/articles/mutualfund/05/mfhistory.asp

Simpson, Stephen. "A Brief History of Exchange-Traded Funds." *Investopedia.com.* Investopedia, 10 Jan. 2012. Web. 7 Feb. 2014.
http://www.investopedia.com/articles/exchangetradedfunds/12/brief-history-exchange-traded-funds.asp

"Wilshire 5000 Index." *Fool.com.* The Motley Fool, n.d. Web. 22 Jan. 2014.
http://www.fool.com/school/indices/wilshire5000.htm

"Wilshire 5000 Total Market Index—TMWX." *Investopedia.com*. Investopedia, n.d. Web. 22 Jan. 2014.
http://www.investopedia.com/terms/w/wilshire5000equityindex.asp

Chapter One: Patterns and Tendencies

None

Chapter Two: Fundamentals

"12B-1 Fee." *Investopedia.com*. Investopedia, n.d. Web. 3 Feb. 2014.
http://www.investopedia.com/terms/1/12b-1fees.asp

Ang, James, and Gregory Nagel. "Outside and Inside Hired CEOs: A Performance Surprise." *Fma.org*. FMA International, n.d. Web. 16 Jan. 2014.
http://www.fma.org/Reno/Papers/Outside_and_Inside_Hired_CEOs_A_-Performance_Surprise_PDDARI.pdf

"Basic Investment Instruments." *aia-pt.com.hk*. AIA, n.d. Web. 12 Jan. 2014.
https://www.aia-pt.com.hk/MPF/en/retirement-planning/investment/

Bostwick, Heleigh. "Top 5 Intellectual Property Disputes." *legalzoom.com*. Legalzoom, Aug. 2009. Web. 10 Jan. 2014.
http://www.legalzoom.com/intellectual-property-rights/intellectual-property-basics/top-5-intellectual-property-disputes

Carlson, Nicholas. "Marissa Mayer Can't Stop Yahoo's Ad Market Share from Slipping." *businessinsider.com*. Business Insider, 19 Dec. 2013. Web. 18 Jan. 2014.
http://www.businessinsider.com/marissa-mayer-cant-stop-yahoos-ad-market-share-from-slipping-2013-12

Chamberlain, Michael. "What's the Difference? Mutual Funds and Exchange Traded Funds Explained." *forbes.com*. Forbes, 18 Jul. 2013. Web. 10 Feb. 2014.

http://www.forbes.com/sites/feeonlyplanner/2013/07/18/whats-the-difference-mutual-funds-and-exchange-traded-funds-explained/

"Chart Pattern." *wikipedia.org.* Wikipedia, n.d. Web. 26 Jan. 2014.
http://en.wikipedia.org/wiki/Chart_pattern

"Chart Patterns." *Stockcharts.com.* Stockcharts.com, n.d. Web. 24 Jan. 2014.
http://stockcharts.com/school/doku.php
?id=chart_school:chart_analysis:chart_patterns

Corrigan, Louis. "How to Read a Mutual Fund Prospectus." *fool.com.* Motley Fool, n.d. Web. 8 Jan. 2014.
https://www.fool.com/School/MutualFunds/Basics/Read.htm

Damato, Karen. "What Exactly Are 12b-1 Fees, Anyway?" *Online.wsj.com.* The Wall Street Journal, 6 Jul. 2010. Web. 7 Feb. 2014.
http://online.wsj.com/news/articles/
SB10001424052748704009804575309011863641700

Davidson, Lee. "The History of Exchange-Traded Funds (ETFs)." *Morningstar.co.uk.* Morningstar, 14 Feb. 2012. Web. 10 Feb. 2014.
http://www.morningstar.co.uk/uk/news/69300/
the-history-of-exchange-traded-funds-(etfs).aspx

"Diversification." *Investopedia.com.* Investopedia, n.d. Web. 14 Feb. 2014.
http://www.investopedia.com/terms/d/diversification.asp

"Diversification (Finance)." *En.wikipedia.org.* Wikipedia, n.d. Web. 14 Feb. 2014.
http://en.wikipedia.org/wiki/Diversification_(finance)

Dizikes, Peter. "Explained: Regression Analysis." *Web.mit.edu.* MIT News, 12 Mar. 2010. Web. 16 Feb. 2014.
http://web.mit.edu/newsoffice/2010/explained-reg-analysis-0316.html

Droge, Kurtis. "7 Things to Think About before Buying a Stock." *wallstcheatsheet.com.* Wall St Cheat Sheet, 7 Nov. 2013. Web. 4 Jan. 2014.

http://wallstcheatsheet.com/stocks/7-things-to-think-about-before-buying-a-stock.html/?a=viewall

"Exchange-Traded Fund—ETF." *Investopedia.com*. Investopedia, n.d. Web. 2 Feb. 2014.
http://www.investopedia.com/terms/e/etf.asp

Gambino, Megan. "Ten Famous Intellectual Property Disputes." *smithsonianmag.com*. Smithsonian.com, 22 Jun. 2011. Web. 10 Jan. 2014.
http://www.smithsonianmag.com/history/ten-famous-intellectual-property-disputes-18521880/

"Introduction to Chart Patterns." *Stockcharts.com*. Stockcharts.com, n.d. Web. 25 Jan. 2014.
http://stockcharts.com/school/doku.php?id=chart_school:chart_analysis:introduction_to_char

Kaplan, David. "Yahoo Management Shakeup Not Worrying Investors, Newspaper Partners—Yet." *gigaom.com*. Gigaom, 30 Sep. 2010. Web. 7 Feb. 2014.
http://paidcontent.org/2010/09/30/419-yahoo-management-shakeup-not-worrying-investors-newspaper-partners-yet/

Little, Ken. "Choosing Business Fundamentals over Management Quality When Investing." *Stock.about.com*. About.com, n.d. Web. 6 Jan. 2014.
http://stocks.about.com/od/investingstrategies/a/Manage121505.htm

Little, Ken. "Look for Companies with Deep Senior Management Talent." *Stocks.about.com*. About.com, n.d. Web. 19 Jan. 2014.
http://stocks.about.com/od/gettingstarted/a/12142012-Look-For-Companies-With-Deep-Senior-Management-Talent.htm

MacMillan, Douglas, and Joann Lubin. "Yahoo's No. 2 Is Out after Clash with CEO Mayer." *Online.wsj.com*. The Wall Street Journal, 15 Jan. 2014. Web. 22 Jan. 2014.

http://online.wsj.com/news/articles/
SB10001424052702304603704579323042547769118?mg=reno64-wsj&
url=http%3A%2F%2Fonline.wsj.com%2Farticle
%2FSB10001424052702304603704579323042547769118.html

"Market School: Japanese Candlesticks—Bullish Three Outside Up." *missingstep.com*. Missing Step Blog, Mar. 2013. Web. 14 Jan. 2014.
http://www.missingstep.com/blog/2013/03/

"More Companies Looking Outside for Their Next CEO." *Conferenceboard.org*. The Conference Board, 1 May 2011. Web. 14 Jan. 2014.
https://www.conference-board.org/press/pressdetail.cfm?pressid=4802

"Mutual Fund Fees and Expenses." *sec.gov*. U.S. Securities and Exchange Commission, n.d. Web. 4 Feb. 2014.
http://www.sec.gov/answers/mffees.htm

"Mutual Funds: The Costs." *Investopedia.com*. Investopedia, n.d. Web. 24 Jan. 2014.
http://www.investopedia.com/university/mutualfunds/mutualfunds2.asp

Nguyen, Joseph. "Regression Basics for Business Analysis." *Investopedia.com*. Investopedia, 4 Aug. 2013. Web. 18 Jan. 2014.
http://www.investopedia.com/articles/financial-theory/09/regression-analysis-basics-business.asp

"The Pros' Guide to Diversification." *Fidelity.com*. Fidelity Investments, 4 Sept. 2013. Web. 14 Feb. 2014.
https://www.fidelity.com/viewpoints/guide-to-diversification

"Raff Regression Channel." *Stockcharts.com*. Stockcharts.com, n.d. Web. 26 Jan. 2014.
http://stockcharts.com/help/doku.php?id=chart_school:chart_analysis:raff_regression_chan

Revell, Janice. "Ten Questions Every Investor Should Ask before Buying a Stock. Before . . ." *Money.cnn.com*. CNNMoney, 22 Dec. 2003. Web. 10 Jan.

2014.
http://money.cnn.com/magazines/fortune/fortune_archive/
2003/12/22/356110/

Schurr, Stephen. "10 Questions to Ask before You Buy a Stock." *thestreet.com.*
The Street, 23 Jan. 2004. Web. 8 Jan. 2014.
http://www.thestreet.com/story/10139093/1/when-to-buy-a-stock.html

"SEC Proposes Measures to Improve Regulation of Fund Distribution Fees
and Provide Better Disclosure for Investor—Press Release." *Sec.gov.* U.S. Securities and Exchange Commission, 21 Jul. 2010. Web. 7 Feb. 2014.
http://www.sec.gov/news/press/2010/2010-126.htm

"Stock-Picking Strategies: Introduction." *Investopedia.com.* Investopedia, 25
Feb. 2009. Web. 14 Jan. 2014.
http://www.investopedia.com/university/stockpicking/

Sykes, Alan. "An Introduction to Regression Analysis." *Law.uchicago.edu.*
University of Chicago, n.d. Web. 12 Jan. 2014.
http://www.law.uchicago.edu/files/files/20.Sykes_.Regression.pdf

"Technical Analysis." *wikipedia.org.* Wikipedia, n.d. Web. 26 Jan. 2014.
http://en.wikipedia.org/wiki/Technical_analysis

"Trend Line (Technical Analysis)." *wikipedia.org.* Wikipedia, n.d. Web. 26
Jan. 2014.
http://en.wikipedia.org/wiki/Trend_line_(technical_analysis)

"Types of Investment Instruments." *ehow.com.* eHow, n.d. Web. 5 Jan. 2014.
http://www.ehow.com/about_5394998_types-investment-instruments.html

"Types of Instruments." *Hsbc.co.in.* HSBC India, n.d. Web. 12 Jan. 2014.
http://www.hsbc.co.in/1/2/personal/investments/new-invest/
new-invest-types

Weisenthal, Joe. "IT'S OFFICIAL: Yahoo Announces That CEO Scott
Thompson Is Out." *businessinsider.com.* Business Insider, 13 Jan. 2012. Web.

8 Jan. 2014.
http://www.businessinsider.com/yahoo-officially-announces-management-shakeup-2012-5

"What Are ETFs?" *nasdaq.com*. NASDAQ, n.d. Web. 10 Feb. 2014.
http://www.nasdaq.com/investing/etfs/what-are-ETFs.aspx

Womack, Brian. "Yahoo CEO Mayer Dismisses Operating Chief De Castro." *businessweek.com*. BloombergBusinessweek, 16 Jan. 2014. Web. 26 Jan. 2014.
http://www.businessweek.com/news/2014-01-15/yahoo-chief-operating-officer-de-castro-to-leave-web-portal

Chapter Three: Registration Types

Anspach, Dana. "2013 Tax Rates—What to Know for Retirement." *Moneyover55.about.com*. About.com, n.d. Web. 8 Jan. 2014.
http://moneyover55.about.com/od/taxtips/ss/2013-Tax-Rates.htm

Appleby, Denise. "Roth IRAs: Distributions." *Investopedia.com*. Investopedia, n.d. Web. 7 Jan. 2014.
http://www.investopedia.com/university/retirementplans/rothira/rothira3.asp

"Capital Gains Tax in the United States." *wikipedia.org*. Wikipedia, n.d. Web. 8 Jan. 2014.
http://en.wikipedia.org/wiki/Capital_gains_tax_in_the_United_States

"Coverdell Education Savings Accounts." *Irs.gov*. IRS, n.d. Web. 28 Jan. 2014.
http://www.irs.gov/uac/Coverdell-Education-Savings-Accounts

Ebeling, Ashlea. "New Tax Law Resurrects Competitor to 529 College Savings Plans." *forbes.com*. Forbes, 14 Jan. 2013. Web. 5 Feb. 2014.
http://www.forbes.com/sites/ashleaebeling/2013/01/14/new-tax-law-resurrects-competitor-to-529-college-savings-plans/

"Federal Capital Gains Tax Rates, 1988-2013." *taxfoundation.org*. Tax Foundation, 13 Jun. 2013. Web. 6 Jan. 2014.
http://taxfoundation.org/article/federal-capital-gains-tax-rates-1988-2013

"The Five Year Rule with Roth IRA Withdrawals." *rothira.com*.
RothIRA.com, 1 Dec. 2011. Web. 17 Feb. 2014.
http://www.rothira.com/blog/the-five-year-rule-with-roth-ira-withdrawals

"An Introduction to 529 Plans." *sec.gov*. U.S. Securities and Exchange Commission, n.d. Web. 9 Feb. 2014.
http://www.sec.gov/investor/pubs/intro529.htm

"Keeping an Eye on the Big Picture." *finra.org*. Finra, n.d. Web. 21 Jan. 2014.
http://www.finra.org/Investors/SmartInvesting/GettingStarted/
BuildingYourPortfolio/P117328

Perez, William. "Capital Gains Tax: Essential Tax Tips for Capital Gains and Losses." *Taxes.about.com*. Publisher of Website, 10 Sep. 2013. Web. 5 Jan. 2014.
http://taxes.about.com/od/capitalgains/a/CapitalGainsTax.htm

Spiegelman, Rande. "Taxes: What's New for 2014?" *schwab.com*. Charles Schwab, 8 Jan. 2014. Web. 29 Jan. 2014.
http://www.schwab.com/public/schwab/resource_center/expert_insight/
schwab_investing_brief/tax_time/taxes_whats_new_now.html

Chapter Four: Electronic Trading and Access to Timely Information

None

Chapter Five: Stock Market Patterns

Best, Ben. "Timing the Market Patterns in American Stock Market Movements." *benbest.com*. Benbest.com, n.d. Web. 6 Feb. 2014.
http://www.benbest.com/business/timing.html

Bouman, Sven, and Ben Jacobsen. "The Halloween Indicator, 'Sell in May and Go Away': Another Puzzle." *American Economic Review*, Dec. 2002, 92(5): 1618-1635.
http://papers.ssrn.com/sol3/papers.cfm?abstract_id=300700##
http://www.aeaweb.org/articles.php?doi=10.1257/000282802762024683

Cekerevac, Sasha. "How True Is the "Sell in May and Go Away" Adage?" *investmentcontrarians.com*. Investment Contrarians, 3 May 2013. Web. 4 Jan. 2014.
http://www.investmentcontrarians.com/stock-market/how-true-is-the-sell-in-may-and-go-away-adage/1967/

Haggard, K. Stephan, and H. Douglas Witte. "Halloween Effect: Trick or Treat?" *International Review of Financial Analysis*, 2010, 19(5).
http://comp.uark.edu/~tjandik/seminar/
Haggard_Witte_Halloween_Effect.pdf

"The Halloween Effect." *Hema.zacks.com*. Zacks, n.d. Web. 11 Jan. 2014.
http://hema.zacks.com/2011/10/the-halloween-effect/

Harding, Sy. "New Academic Study Says Seasonality Triples Market Returns over Long-Term!" *streetsmartreport.com*. Asset Management Research Corp, 5 Oct. 2012. Web. 25 Jan. 2014.
http://www.streetsmartreport.com/school/Commentaries/
New%20Study%20Says%20'Sell%20in%20May'%20Triples%20Markets%20
Gains%20Long-Term.html

Hirsch, Jeffrey. "Using Seasonal and Cyclical Stock Market Patterns." *aaii.com*. AAII Journal, Jun. 2013. Web. 19 Jan. 2014.
http://www.aaii.com/journal/article/using-seasonal-and-cyclical-stock-market-patterns.mobile

Hulbert, Mark. "Is the Santa Claus Rally for Real? Wall Street Likes to Say So. Don't Fall for Their Pales pitch." *Online.wsj.com*. The Wall Street Journal, 29 Nov. 2013. Web. 25 Jan. 2014.

http://online.wsj.com/news/articles/
SB10001424052702304281004579221941937294668

Jacobsen, Ben, and Nuttawat Visaltanachoti. "The Halloween Effect in US Sectors." *The Financial Review*, 8 May 2006.
http://papers.ssrn.com/sol3/papers.cfm?abstract_id=901088

Jacobsen, Ben, and Cherry Yi Zhang. "The Halloween Indicator: Everywhere and All the Time." Social Science Research Network, 1 Oct. 2012.
http://www.cfainstitute.org/learning/products/publications/contributed/
Pages/the_halloween_indicator__everywhere_and_all_the_time.aspx

Larrabee, David. "The Halloween Indicator: A Stock Market Anomaly That Is Stronger Than Ever." *blogs.cfainstitute.org*. CFA Institute, 30 Oct. 2012. Web. 25 Jan. 2014.
http://blogs.cfainstitute.org/investor/2012/10/30/the-halloween-indicator-a-stock-market-anomaly-that-is-stronger-than-ever/

Learnvest, Staff. "Does 'Sell in May and Go Away' Actually Work?" *thefinancialtimes.com*. The Financial Times, 31 May 2013. Web. 15 Jan. 2014.
http://www.thefiscaltimes.com/Articles/2013/05/31/Does-Sell-in-May-and-Go-Away-Actually-Work

Malkiel, Burton. "The Efficient Market Hypothesis and Its Critics." *Emlab.berkeley.edu*. Berkeley University, n.d. Web. 23 Jan. 2014.
http://emlab.berkeley.edu/~craine/EconH195/Fall_13/webpage/
Malkiel_Efficient%20Mkts.pdf

Nesto, Matt. " Sell in May and Go Where? Preparing for the Market's Slow Season." *Finance.yahoo.com*. Yahoo, 30 Apr. 2013. Web. 8 Jan. 2014.
http://finance.yahoo.com/blogs/breakout/sell-may-where-preparing-market
-slow-season-111749068.html

Parets, J.C. "Sell in May and Go Away?" *allstarcharts.com*. All Star Charts, 25 Apr. 2013. Web. 11 Jan. 2014.
http://allstarcharts.com/sell-in-may-and-go-away-2/

"Program Trading." *wikipedia.org*. Wikipedia, n.d. Web. 23 Jan. 2014.
http://en.wikipedia.org/wiki/Program_trading

"Santa Claus Rally." *Investopedia.com*. Investopedia, n.d. Web. 12 Jan. 2014.
http://www.investopedia.com/terms/s/santaclauseffect.asp

"Sell in May." *wikipedia.org*. Wikipedia, n.d. Web. 12 Jan. 2014.
http://en.wikipedia.org/wiki/Sell_in_May

"Sell In May and Go Away." *Investopedia.com*. Investopedia, n.d. Web. 12
Jan. 2014.
http://www.investopedia.com/terms/s/sell-in-may-and-go-away.asp

Swanson, Mike. "The Seasonal December Stock Market Rally Trend Is Real."
howestreet.com. HowStreet.com, 8 Dec. 2011. Web. 25 Jan. 2014.
http://howestreet.com/2011/12/the-seasonal-december-stock-market-rally-
trend-is-real/

Chapter Six: Forces Creating Patterns

Athanassakos, George, and Lucy Ackert. "The Seasonal Impact of Institutional Investors [The January Effect]." *Bengrahaminvesting.ca*. Ben Graham
Investing, Fall 1998. Web. 10 Jan. 2014.
http://www.bengrahaminvesting.ca/Research/Papers/Athanassakos/
The_Seasonal_Impact_of_Institutional_Investors.pdf

Bruno, Maria, and Stephen Weber. "Do You Max?" *vanguardblog.com*. Vanguard, 1 Nov. 2013. Web. 11 Feb. 2014.
http://vanguardblog.com/2013/11/01/do-you-max/

Choe, Stan. "Managers Make Case for Investing in Own Funds." *boston-
globe.com*. Associated Press, 21 Sep. 2013. Web. 5 Feb. 2014.
http://www.bostonglobe.com/business/2013/09/20/only-some-mutual-fund
-managers-invest-their-own/ULInqyKo1NTJXdoJHvO1cL/story.html

"Excess Contributions." *Irs.gov.* IRS, n.d. Web. 2 Feb. 2014.
http://www.irs.gov/publications/p571/ch07.html

"Frequently Asked Questions about Taxation for Mutual Fund Investors."
Ici.org. ICI Global, Dec. 2013. Web. 5 Feb. 2014.
http://www.ici.org/policy/current_issues/faqs_taxation_investors

"January Effect." *wikipedia.org.* Wikipedia, n.d. Web. 30 Jan. 2014.
http://en.wikipedia.org/wiki/January_effect

Kenny, Thomas. "Why You Shouldn't Buy Mutual Funds before They Pay
Distributions." *Bonds.about.com.* About.com, n.d. Web. 27 Jan. 2014.
http://bonds.about.com/od/bondfunds/fl/Why-You-Shouldnrsquot-Buy-
Mutual-Funds-Before-They-Pay-Dividends.htm

Kinnel, Russel. "Do Managers Eat Their Own Cooking?" *morningstar.com.*
Morningstar, n.d. Web. 8 Feb. 2014.
http://www.morningstar.com/products/pdf/MFIMWEOC0608.pdf

Marte, Jonnelle. "Delaying IRA Contributions Can Be Costly."
Online.wsj.com. The Wall Street Journal, 16 Jan. 2014. Web. 11 Feb. 2014.
http://online.wsj.com/news/articles/
SB10001424052702304477704579256610849790176

Quinlan, Casey. "Should Managers Invest in Their Own Mutual Funds?"
Money.usnews.com. U.S. News & World Report, 8 Nov. 2013. Web. 2 Feb.
2014.
http://money.usnews.com/money/personal-finance/mutual-funds/articles/
2013/11/08/should-managers-invest-in-their-own-mutual-funds

Quinn, Laura. "First Person: Why I Fund My Roth IRA Early in the Year."
Finance.yahoo.com. Yahoo, 21 Jan. 2014. Web. 12 Feb. 2014.
http://finance.yahoo.com/news/first-person-why-fund-roth-ira-early-
195400352–finance.html

Zweig, Jason, and Tom McGinty. "Fund Managers Lift Results with Timely
Trading Sprees." *Online.wsj.com.* The Wall Street Journal, 6 Dec. 2012. Web.

11 Feb. 2014.
http://online.wsj.com/news/articles/
SB10001424127887324205404578147190736344284

Chapter Seven: The Tactics within Sound Investment Strategies

Barnes, Ryan. "Economic Indicators: Mutual Fund Flows." *Investopedia.com.*
Investopedia, n.d. Web. 27 Jan. 2014.
http://www.investopedia.com/university/releases/mutualfundflows.asp

Burrows, Dan. "5 Great Dividend Mutual Funds." *investorplace.com.* InvestorPlace, 7 Aug. 2013. Web. 5 Feb. 2014.
http://investorplace.com/2013/08/5-great-dividend-mutual-funds/#.UvaUw-Plr58E

Choe, Stan. "The Mutual Fund Fee That May Be Good for You."
news.gnom.es. Gnomes National News Service,
25 Jan. 2014. Web. 10 Feb. 2014.
http://news.gnom.es/news/the-mutual-fund-fee-that-may-be-good-for-you

"Defensive Stock." *Investopedia.com.* Investopedia, n.d. Web. 5 Feb. 2014.
http://www.investopedia.com/terms/d/defensivestock.asp

"Defensive Stock." *investorwords.com.* InvestorWords, n.d. Web. 5 Feb. 2014.
http://www.investorwords.com/5500/defensive_stock.html

"Double Your Money: The Rule of 72." *accountingcoach.com.* Accounting Coach, n.d. Web. 1 Feb. 2014.
http://www.accountingcoach.com/future-value-of-a-single-amount/explanation/8

"Investing Your Money Basics." *money.cnn.com.* CNNMoney, n.d. Web. 9 Jan. 2014.
http://money.cnn.com/magazines/moneymag/money101/lesson4/

Mohindra, Amit. "The Rule of 72." *Nelsontouchconsulting.wordpress.com.* The Nelson Touch Blog, 28 Feb. 2011. Web. 1 Feb. 2014.
http://nelsontouchconsulting.wordpress.com/2011/02/28/the-rule-of-72/

"Morningstar Investing Glossary: Redemption Fee." *morningstar.com.* Morningstar, n.d. Web. 14 Feb. 2014.
http://www.morningstar.com/InvGlossary/redemption_fee.aspx

"Net Asset Value Transfers: Look before You Leap into Another Mutual Fund." *finra.org.* FINRA, n.d. Web. 10 Feb. 2014.
https://www.finra.org/Investors/ProtectYourself/InvestorAlerts/
MutualFunds/p005963

"Rebalancing Investments." *wikipedia.org.* Wikipedia, n.d. Web. 1 Feb. 2014.
http://en.wikipedia.org/wiki/Rebalancing_investments

Federal Reserve Interest Rate Interactive Chart. *tradingeconomics.com.* Trading Economics, n.d. Web. 10 Jan. 2014.
http://www.tradingeconomics.com/united-states/interest-rate

Vohwinkle, Jeremy. "Using the Rule of 72 to Estimate Investment Returns." *financialplan.about.com.* About.com, n.d. Web. 1 Feb. 2014.
http://financialplan.about.com/od/personalfinance/qt/Ruleof72.htm

"Redemption Fee." *Investopedia.com.* Investopedia, n.d. Web. 7 Feb. 2014.
http://www.investopedia.com/terms/r/redemptionfee.asp

"Redemption Fees." *smart401k.com.* Smart401K, n.d. Web. 7 Feb. 2014.
http://www.smart401k.com/Content/retail/resource-center/
retirement-investing-basics/redemption-fees